Management Extra

LEADERSHIP AND MANAGEMENT IN ORGANISATIONS

ELSEVIER

eLEARN

Pergamon
Flexible
Learning

AMSTERDAM • BOSTON • HEIDELBERG • LONDON • NEW YORK • OXFORD • PARIS •
SAN DIEGO • SAN FRANCISCO • SINGAPORE • SYDNEY • TOKYO

Pergamon Flexible Learning is an imprint of Elsevier
Linacre House, Jordan Hill, Oxford OX2 8DP, UK
30 Corporate Drive, Suite 400, Burlington, MA 01803, USA

First edition 2007

British Library Cataloguing in Publication Data
A catalogue record for this book is available from the British Library

Library of Congress Cataloging-in-Publication Data
A catalog record for this book is available from the Library of Congress

ISBN: 978-0-08-046528-9

For information on all Pergamon Flexible Learning publications visit
our web site at books.elsevier.com

Printed and bound in Italy

07 08 09 10 11 10 9 8 7 6 5 4 3 2 1

Contents

Activities

Figures

Tables

Series preface

Whether you are a tutor/trainer or studying management development to further your career, Management Extra provides an exciting and flexible resource helping you to achieve your goals. The series is completely new and up-to-date, and has been written to harmonise with the 2004 national occupational standards in management and leadership. It has also been mapped to management qualifications, including the Institute of Leadership & Management's middle and senior management qualifications at Levels 5 and 7 respectively on the revised national framework.

For learners, coping with all the pressures of today's world, Management Extra offers you the flexibility to study at your own pace to fit around your professional and other commitments. Suddenly, you don't need a PC or to attend classes at a specific time – choose when and where to study to suit yourself! And, you will always have the complete workbook as a quick reference just when you need it.

For tutors/trainers, Management Extra provides an invaluable guide to what needs to be covered, and in what depth. It also allows learners who miss occasional sessions to 'catch up' by dipping into the series.

This series provides unrivalled support for all those involved in management development at middle and senior levels.

Reviews of Management Extra

I have utilised the Management Extra series for a number of Institute of Leadership and Management (ILM) Diploma in Management programmes. The series provides course tutors with the flexibility to run programmes in a variety of formats, from fully facilitated, using a choice of the titles as supporting information, to a tutorial based programme, where the complete series is provided for home study. These options also give course participants the flexibility to study in a manner which suits their personal circumstances. The content is interesting, thought provoking and up-to-date, and, as such, I would highly recommend the use of this series to suit a variety of individual and business needs.

Martin Davies BSc(Hons) MEd CEngMIMechE MCIPD FITOL FInstLM
Senior Lecturer, University of Wolverhampton Business School

At last, the complete set of books that make it all so clear and easy to follow for tutor and student. A must for all those taking middle/senior management training seriously.

Michael Crothers, ILM National Manager

Management and leadership in organisations

John Kotter of the Harvard Business School is one of a number of experts who believe that organisations are over managed and under led, at least partially because people do not appreciate the differences between management and leadership.

We start this book by asking you to challenge your mental models of leadership and management. In the literature, models for leadership and management are evolving all the time, yet mostly we base our thinking about what does or doesn't work on our personal experience. The consequence is that it is easy to become trapped in a particular style and way of working, and to rely on the same strategies to get us through very different situations.

Agility has become a prerequisite for organisations in a business environment that is characterised by change. The implications for management and leadership have been profound. Two trends in particular have been evident.

> First hierarchical systems of management are yielding to a 'new leadership' movement which has at its core shared vision and individual empowerment in place of consistency and control. Second, leadership is no longer the preserve of those in positions in the management hierarchy. Increasingly it is dispersed through the organisation. There are now many who have a responsibility for leading and managing in some form.

By developing your awareness of these and other influential trends, you will be better equipped to flex your style and to play the diverse roles required of the managerial leader in contemporary organisations. In this book you explore the changing nature of organisations and assess what this means for the leadership role.

> Your objectives are to:
>
> ◆ use contemporary concepts and theories to analyse your approach to management and leadership and to identify areas for development
>
> ◆ review how organisational structures are changing to enable organisations to become more agile and responsive to their stakeholders
>
> ◆ evaluate the culture of your organisation and team and assess what this means for effective management practice

- improve your influencing skills and the level of influence you hold with organisational stakeholders

- explore ways in which you can build a culture of commitment, performance and learning.

1 Essentials of leadership and management

As a concept leadership has been around for thousands of years. In contrast, management science, driven by the phenomenon of large organisations and the need to bring order and consistency to their functioning, only emerged during the 20th century.

Leadership is different from management, but not for the reasons most people think. Leadership isn't mystical and mysterious. It is not necessarily to do with being exceptionally brilliant or charismatic. It is not the province of a chosen few. Nor is leadership better than management or a replacement for it. Without good management, complex enterprises tend to become chaotic in ways that threaten their very existence.

In this theme, you will:

♦ explore the relationship between leadership and management in contemporary organisations

♦ identify the diverse roles of the modern manager and explore your strengths and preferences

♦ explore why leaders need to be self-aware and practice techniques to develop self-awareness.

What is the relationship between management and leadership?

Recently there has been a surge of interest in leadership and it has been driven by a number of factors:

♦ **The information age** has had a profound effect on the workings of organisations. Information and knowledge are now readily available to all of us who bother to seek it out. Successful managers are no longer characterised by what they know but how they create a culture that enables people to achieve their true potential.

♦ **Globalisation** has resulted in diversity in its widest sense. To maximise contribution, managers are now challenged with creating inclusive working environments. They need to understand cultural perceptions of leadership and to deploy a wide variety of leadership styles to build trust and effective working relationships.

♦ **Organisations have become flatter** reducing the number of managers and increasing their span of control. People on the front line now have greater responsibility for decision making and directing their own activities. With greater empowerment comes the need for strong values and a shared vision to help people make the right choices.

♦ **Rapid economic and technological change** in the external environment poses new opportunities and threats to the organisation and therefore to the leaders in organisations. How can they handle such turbulence and steer the organisation to success?

As organisations have struggled to meet these challenges, there has been growing recognition that management science, with its focus on control and consistency, is inadequate. Doing what was done yesterday, or doing it 5% better, is no longer a formula for success. Organisations need to become better skilled at creating leaders of people and change.

There have been many attempts to isolate leadership attributes from management attributes. The following model from Warren Bennis (1989) is a classic example.

The Manager	The Leader
Administers	Innovates
Maintains	Develops
Relies on control	Inspires people
Shorter range view	Longer range view
Asks how and when	Asks what and why
Accepts the status quo	Challenges it
Does things right	Does the right thing

Table 1.1 *Managers and leaders (Bennis,1989)*

For many, the distinction between leaders and managers is more confusing than it is informative. It implies that people are either one of the other. More helpful is to think of leadership and management as distinctive and complementary processes rather than as positions. Leadership then becomes one of the roles that managers need to be able to play (Mintzberg, 1973).

To sum up the distinction, management is about coping with complexity. It brings a degree of order and consistency to technical dimensions like the quality and profitability of products (Kotter, 2001). Leadership, by contrast, is about relationships. It is about being able to influence people to behave in a desired manner (Bennis, 1989) and is fundamental to change. Both are necessary for success. The most successful firms will combine strong leadership with effective management and will seek to develop the potential of their people in both areas.

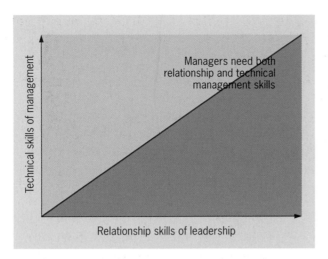

Figure 1.1 *Management and leadership as roles*

In this book you focus primarily on the relationship aspects of being a manager and in particular on the process of leadership. Other books in the Management Extra series explore more technical management skills including finance, quality and project management.

The eight roles of the managerial leader

Robert Quinn (2002) argues that managers can become trapped in their own style with the consequence that they use the same strategies in very different situations. He is among a number of authors who argue that managers need to equip themselves to play a broad range of management and leadership roles.

> **For managers the world keeps changing. It changes from hour to hour, day to day and week to week. The strategies that were effective yesterday are not necessarily effective in the same situation today.**
> **Quinn (2002)**

Consider the following:

Paul had graduated from a five year bio-engineering programme in four years and took a job with a small family owned company. Starting out brilliantly he quickly became their star performer and as the company grew he was promoted rapidly. He had an ability to take a complex technical problem and come up with a better answer than anyone else, faster than anyone else. He was also hard-driving, pushing his people to accomplish some pretty impressive tasks.

After three years Paul was headhunted to become Director of Research with an international competitor. He was given a crack team and a budget to match. But the next couple of years were difficult for him. For the first time he received negative feedback about his performance. His team often rejected his ideas and three key members left. Reflecting on his time, he said:

> 'It was awful. They were always making what I thought were the wrong decisions and when I pointed out the right solution, they either argued or ignored me.'

Paul was less successful than he might have been because of his beliefs about what a leader is supposed to do. For him, good management meant being a tough leader who makes the decisions. His model was not completely wrong but it was inadequate for his new organisation and team.

Experience and practice within an organisation can mean that managers become naturally stronger at some management roles than others.

> 'Coca-Cola's biggest brand launch in Britain for decades, the sugar-free drink Coke Zero, may be in danger of failing. After an initial burst, aided by hot weather and a huge marketing campaign that aroused the public's curiosity, sales of Coke Zero appear to have suffered sizeable falls. It is not only at the hands of consumers that Coca-Cola has suffered. On Wall Street, the once mighty company has fallen into the shadow of PepsiCo, its fierce rival which has won plaudits for its rapid diversification into healthier soft drinks and water products. Coca-Cola by contrast has been attacked for its ponderous product development and failure to adapt to changing consumer demands.'

Source: Abridged from the Sunday Times, 27th August 2006

Coca-Cola regularly ranks near the top of listings of global brands. It is a company that is renowned for consistency in its production and distribution systems and where managers have traditionally been under continuous pressure to show improvement in product volumes and profits. Jobs have literally been won or lost over small differences in bottom line indicators as it has battled with PepsiCo for global dominance.

Now both companies find themselves in a different market position, one where their longer term survival is threatened by the declining consumption of traditional fizzy drinks. To increase their dominant positions within the marketplace, they need to innovate and respond to changing consumer preference. But at the same time, they need to maintain their foothold in their core marketplace.

The Coca-Cola scenario illustrates how we can have conflicting expectations of organisations and their managers. On the one hand we expect them to be stable and to devote attention to their people and internal processes, but on the other we want them to be adaptive and to respond to pressures coming from the external environment.

Being able to respond to these competing expectations is a vital and challenging management task.

Managers need to balance competing demands

Quinn identifies eight management roles in his competing values framework (Figure 1.2), so named because each role places demands on the manager that compete with the one that lies opposite to it in the circle.

Take the producer (goal oriented) and facilitator (relationship focused) roles for example. Some of us will have worked for a manager, or for an organisation, where attainment of goals and outcomes was the priority, at the expense of healthy working relationships. Others will have the opposite experience where managers are prepared to compromise on goals to keep their team happy. In reality managers need to focus on goals and people.

Or the innovator and co-ordinator roles. In some organisations, tasks have become so standardised and routine that co-ordination is key and dynamic innovative leadership qualities seem almost redundant. But in reality, as in the Coca-Cola example, all organisations need the capacity to innovate and adapt.

Your experience and personality mean that you're likely to be stronger in some of the roles than others. Along the way you might also have come to believe that some roles are more important than others. If you accept Quinn's thinking, then this is something you need to question. Quinn maintains that performing well as a managerial leader within our diverse and changing world means being competent across all roles and learning to balance them.

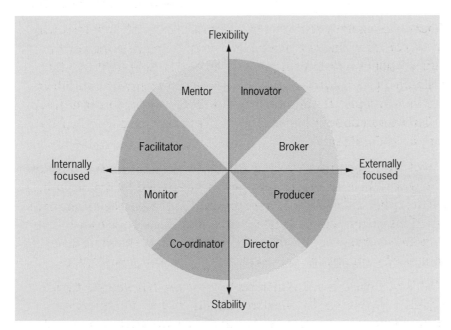

Figure 1.2 *The Competing Values Framework*
Source: Adapted from Becoming a Master Manager, Quinn (2002)

The roles of a managerial leader	Values	Competences
The **innovator** is creative and facilitates adaptation and change.	Innovation Adaptation	◆ Living with change ◆ Thinking creatively ◆ Managing change
The **broker** is politically astute, persuasive, influential, and powerful, and is particularly concerned with maintaining the organisation's external legitimacy and obtaining external resources.	Growth Resource acquisition	◆ Building and maintaining a powerbase ◆ Negotiating agreement and commitment ◆ Presenting ideas
The **mentor** is helpful and approachable, and engages in the development of people through a caring, empathetic orientation.	Morale Commitment	◆ Understanding self and others ◆ Communicating effectively ◆ Developing employees
The **facilitator** encourages teamwork and cohesiveness, and manages interpersonal conflict.	Participation Openness	◆ Building teams ◆ Using participative decision making ◆ Managing conflict
The **monitor** checks on performance and handles paperwork.	Information management Documentation	◆ Monitoring individual performance ◆ Managing collective performance ◆ Analysing information with critical thinking
The **co-ordinator** maintains structure, schedules, organises and co-ordinates peoples' work.	Stability Control	◆ Managing projects ◆ Designing work ◆ Managing across functions
The **director** engages in planning and goal setting, sets objectives and establishes clear expectations.	Direction Goal clarity	◆ Developing and communicating a vision ◆ Setting goals and objectives ◆ Designing and organising
The **producer** is task-oriented and work-focused, and motivates members to increase production and to accomplish stated goals.	Accomplishment Productivity	◆ Working productively ◆ Fostering a productive work environment ◆ Managing time and stress

Table 1.2 *Leadership roles and competencies from the competing values framework*

Applying the framework at different management levels

Although Quinn's management roles are not tied to any particular level of manager, the responsibilities and behaviours that are expected do vary as you move through the hierarchy.

All managers perform the monitor role for example, but with different nuances and objectives. First-level managers use short range scheduling, expense budgets, operations management, and measurement tools to oversee the activities of their team. Senior managers are engaged more in evaluating financial statements and reports, and are concerned with control systems that measure performance and profit at the organisation level. Middle managers, on the other hand use control systems to monitor the activities of lower levels and to support intermediate planning. You will need to interpret the model in the context of your own role.

The managerial leader

Earlier we highlighted the value of leadership and management as complementary processes in the management toolkit. Quinn's framework helps us to organise this thinking into a profile that shows what a managerial leader should do.

If we take the Director role for instance, the technical managerial tasks of *Setting goals and objectives* and *Designing and organising* are set alongside the competence of *Developing and communicating a vision*, an essential factor in leading change.

Some roles might be more uniquely management (monitor and co-ordinator) or leadership (innovator), but overall the framework reflects both, helping to make clear how leadership can be discharged alongside the administrative aspects of management within the modern organisation.

Activity 1
The roles of the managerial leader

Objective

The following questionnaire reflects some of the key behaviours that a manager will perform in each of the management roles. You can use it as a frame of reference to reflect on your own management style.

Task

1. For each of the following statements rate your effectiveness

How effectively do you:	Ineffective		Very effective		
	1	2	3	4	5
1. maintain a high level of personal energy, motivation and effort	☐	☐	☐	☐	☐
2. set and prioritise goals	☐	☐	☐	☐	☐
3. focus on achieving results	☐	☐	☐	☐	☐
4. involve others in decision making	☐	☐	☐	☐	☐
5. make tough and important decisions	☐	☐	☐	☐	☐
6. support imposed change even when you don't agree with it	☐	☐	☐	☐	☐
7. schedule workflow for tasks and people	☐	☐	☐	☐	☐
8. adjust workloads and reallocate resources when needed	☐	☐	☐	☐	☐
9. network with people external to the organisation	☐	☐	☐	☐	☐
10. disseminate information about policies and procedures	☐	☐	☐	☐	☐
11. allocate resources to tasks and projects	☐	☐	☐	☐	☐
12. motivate others	☐	☐	☐	☐	☐
13. anticipate problems in projects	☐	☐	☐	☐	☐
14. collect and interpret data to monitor performance	☐	☐	☐	☐	☐
15. manage inter-personal conflict in the team	☐	☐	☐	☐	☐
16. act as an advocate for your team or unit to others in the organisation	☐	☐	☐	☐	☐
17. interpret financial and statistical reports	☐	☐	☐	☐	☐
18. set-up systems to support the flow of information around the team and with other teams	☐	☐	☐	☐	☐
19. seek commitment to goals from team	☐	☐	☐	☐	☐
20. assess potential impact of change proposals	☐	☐	☐	☐	☐
21. gives credit to people for their work	☐	☐	☐	☐	☐
22. maintain an open and approachable attitude to people in your team	☐	☐	☐	☐	☐
23. define roles and expectations of people	☐	☐	☐	☐	☐
24. come up with ideas to improve the organisation	☐	☐	☐	☐	☐
25. exert influence upwards and sideways	☐	☐	☐	☐	☐
26. create opportunities for people to challenge and develop themselves	☐	☐	☐	☐	☐
27. create high performance expectations in others	☐	☐	☐	☐	☐
28. involve subordinates in work planning	☐	☐	☐	☐	☐
29. coach and do on-the-job training	☐	☐	☐	☐	☐
30. create a sense of teamwork	☐	☐	☐	☐	☐
31. encourage creativity within the team	☐	☐	☐	☐	☐
32. build networks and coalitions within the organisation	☐	☐	☐	☐	☐

2. Plot your scores onto the matrix below

Role	Question number	Score	Question number	Score	Question number	Score	Question number	Score	Total
Innovator	6		20		24		31		
Broker	9		16		25		32		
Producer	1		3		12		27		
Director	2		5		19		23		
Co-ordinator	7		8		11		13		
Monitor	10		14		17		18		
Facilitator	15		21		22		30		
Mentor	26		29		30		31		

3. What did you learn about your leadership style and performance?
   Which roles do you fulfill? Where do you focus your time? What kind of
   manager are you today?

4. What do you need to work on in order to become a more effective
   managerial leader?

Feedback

Just thinking about your management approach is a useful start for your development. One of the recurring themes of this book is that to understand others, you as a manager must start by understanding yourself.

Your personality and experience will mean that naturally you are stronger at some roles than others. The organisational environment in which you currently work or have worked in previously might also have led you to value some roles as being more important than others.

Quinn emphasises that learning to perform well means becoming competent across all roles and learning to balance them rather than excelling in any one of them. 'A person might become so committed to the behaviour in one role, that he or she loses touch with the opposite. This might make a normally effective person ineffective.'

Quinn's competing values framework is one of a number of models that describe the roles a manager should play. For different perspectives you might want to look at the work of Henry Mintzberg and also at the management standards (The Management Standards Centre). You can find references in the More@ section at the end of this theme.

Developing as a leader

'In a few hundred years, when the history of our time will be written from a long-term perspective, it is likely that the most important event historians will see is not technology, not the Internet, not e-commerce. It is an unprecedented change in the human condition. For the first time – literally – substantial and rapidly growing numbers of people have choices. For the first time, they will have to manage themselves. And society is totally unprepared for it.'

Source: Peter Drucker (2000)

Peter Drucker one of the world's foremost authorities on leadership and management argues that in today's 'age of opportunity' people must learn to manage and to develop themselves.

He argues that to do this effectively we need first to cultivate a deep understanding of ourselves – of our strengths and weaknesses, how we learn, how we work with others, what our values are and how we best perform. Only when we have this understanding, often referred to as self-awareness, are we able to place ourselves where we are able to make the greatest contribution.

> **One quality of leaders and high achievers in every area seems to be a commitment to ongoing personal and professional development.**
> **Brian Tracy, motivation coach and author**

What is self-awareness?

So what do we mean when we talk about self-awareness? Do we have a single, central self? The answer is yes and no. We have seen already that we offer different facets of ourselves in various roles and situations. Some of these facets will be more authentic or natural than others and understanding these can help you to become more aware, at a conscious level of yourself.

Take a piece of paper and make a list of ten or more attributes that you consider to be your strengths. Do you for example, consider yourself to be courageous, innovative, thoughtful, ambitious, lively, charismatic, considerate?

> **If you do not understand yourself, it is virtually impossible to understand others.**
> **Quinn (2002)**

You might think you know instinctively what you are good at, yet few people actually step back and question their assumptions. Researchers in the area claim that in reality people are more aware of what they are not good at with the consequence that most people plan their development around their weaknesses. In reality high performers tend to operate from their natural strengths, so optimising these is as, if not more, important than developing your weaknesses.

You may already feel that you have a high level of self-awareness. On the other hand you might sometimes find yourself questioning why you acted or felt as you did in certain situations. By continuously developing your self-awareness you can gain more control over your behaviour. This in turn can improve the way you work with people, for example when coaching, giving feedback, reviewing performance and resolving problems.

The power of reflection

Reflecting on your past experiences is one of the best ways to get to know yourself better. Think for a moment about what you might learn by spending a year in two very different environments: managing a voluntary project overseas or as a supervisor of a building site construction crew. Each offers different leadership challenges and both offer a rich store for learning about yourself as a leader, the situations in which you thrive and those you find challenging. You could however, just as easily spend your time in either environment and learn nothing.

Learning experts point out that leadership development depends not just on the kinds of experience you have but also on your ability to use them to gain self-awareness and personal growth. They believe people learn more from their experience when they take time to think about them.

Learning from experience essentially involves three different processes; action, observation and reflection. If we act but do not observe the consequences of our action or reflect on its significance and meaning, then it makes little sense to say we have learnt from the experience.

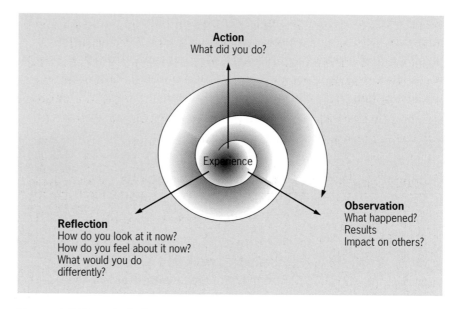

Figure 1.3 *The spiral of experience (adapted from Hughes, Ginnet and Curphy)*

Learning through reflection

In *A Manager's Guide to Self Development*, Pedlar et al. identify three elements that influence your behaviour in any incident.

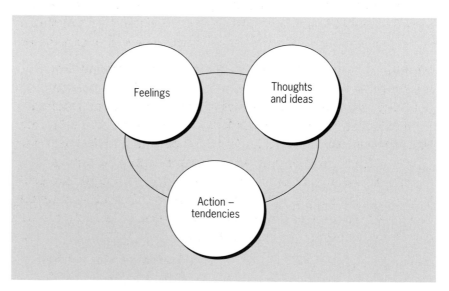

Figure 1.4 *Determinants of behaviour*

To show the interplay between the three areas, they cite the example of a manager in a meeting. During the meeting a senior manager expressed a viewpoint which the chair supported but with which our manager – who was more junior – disagreed. Our manager's thoughts / ideas were that what had been said was fundamentally wrong. His feelings were mixed. On the one hand, he felt concern and excitement to get his viewpoint across. On the other he felt a more deep-rooted fear of ridicule and challenging authority. His previous experience suggested he was likely to be shot down and so his natural action-tendency in this kind of situation was to say nothing.

His behaviour in this situation will depend on which of the three elements wins out. Will his ideas and feelings of concern and excitement overcome his natural action tendency? Or will his fears lead him to succumb to his natural action tendency and remain silent? Or will his feelings and action tendencies result in a fumbling presentation of ideas? Table 1.2 provides us with a framework for analysing our response to critical events.

Responses	Before the event	During the event	After the event
My feelings			
My thoughts / ideas			
My action-tendencies			
My actual behaviour			

Table 1.3 *Critical incident analysis*

Your feelings, thoughts/ideas and action tendencies are all interconnected and triggered in response to a particular stimulus, e.g. the presence of the authority figure in the meeting. Understanding the stimulus that triggers certain types of behaviour provides you with an opportunity to think what different or similar action you could take when faced with the same sort of experience.

It's as important to reflect on incidents that have gone well as it is on those that have proved challenging. While there is no doubting that experience provides insights and wisdom, research from Ashridge Business School (2005) shows that the crucial factor that determines how well a leader will cope with a critical incident in the future is whether they have the confidence and coping mechanisms from having weathered similarly challenging incidents in the past. Put simply you are more likely to succeed if you have a good understanding of how you react in difficult situations and the confidence to believe that you will cope.

Activity 2
Reflection as a learning technique

Objective

Use this activity to practice the skills of reflection.

Task

1. Identify a co-worker with whom you have frequent interaction and with whom you would like to improve your relationship.

2. Now think about one or two significant incidents that have recently occurred between you. Any significant incident(s) from which you can draw conclusions can provide you with an insight into your behaviour. Try to recall your feelings, thoughts and ideas, action-tendencies and behaviours. Note them down below.

Responses	Before the event	During the event	After the event
My feelings			
My thoughts / ideas			
My action-tendencies			
My actual behaviour			

3. What does this event tell you about yourself ? What would help you to work with your co-worker more effectively?

4. Imagine you are preparing for a feedback session with your co-worker. Prepare a list of questions and prompts for the session.

Feedback

This way of analysing relationships and incidents should become part of your everyday managerial life and throughout this book there are plenty of opportunities to develop your skills. By continuously developing your self-awareness you can gain more control over your behaviour and enhance your understanding of others. Be sure to reflect on successful incidents as well as those that you have found difficult. This will help you to build self-confidence as a leader and to ensure you use your strengths to the full.

One shortcoming of reflection as a learning technique is that it doesn't necessarily involve another person, so there is no challenge to your thinking, your assumptions, logic or conclusions. Feedback from a 'critical friend' is one way to overcome this. As a manager, you need to act as a role model by being open to external feedback in order to develop an environment in which those you work with are also encouraged to seek and value feedback. There are many opportunities throughout this book where you'll find it helpful to seek feedback on how you can develop as a leader.

Models of leadership

Type leadership into your search engine and you'll find that there are very many ways to finish the sentence 'Leadership is...'

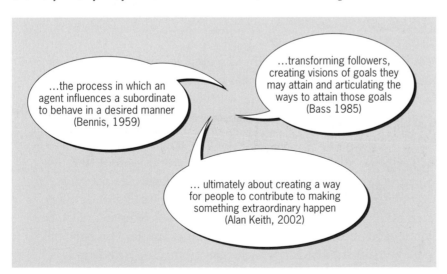

Figure 1.5 *Perspectives on leadership*

Much research has been focused on what makes a leader tick. Understanding some of this can help you develop and adapt your own leadership style and so become a more effective leader. In this section you explore the leadership role and some of the main theories that have developed around it.

Being a leader

To start you thinking about leadership, identify someone that you work with who has good leadership skills. What characteristics do you particularly admire?

Kouzes and Posner (2002) have spent the past twenty years researching the **leadership traits** that people look for and most value. From over 75,000 responses, they have compiled the following list.

> Ambitious, broad-minded, caring, co-operative, competent, courageous, dependable, determined, fair-minded, forward-looking, honest, imaginative, independent, inspiring, intelligence, loyal, mature, self-controlled, straightforward, supportive.

Four key traits have topped their list.

	What values do you look for and admire in your leaders? (% of respondents citing character)		
	2002	1995	1987
Honest	88	88	83
Forward looking	71	75	62
Competent	66	63	67
Inspiring	65	68	58

While interesting, the problem in seeing leadership in terms of personality traits is that it implies certain people are born to be leaders and as such, offers little to developing managers. Personality is hard to change but the evidence suggests that leadership is a skill that people can learn and improve.

Behavioural studies are more useful as a development tool. By isolating how effective managers behave, it becomes possible to provide managers with a framework to evaluate and develop their performance. Quinn's Competing Values Framework that you looked at earlier in this section is an example. The national management standards (www.management-standards.org) is another. Many organisations have developed their own frameworks of management competence to meet the needs of their business and the context in which they operate.

The right style for the right situation

Researchers achieve varied results when they try to isolate the behaviours of effective leaders. This is understandable. The most fitting leadership style will vary according to the situation and a good leader will find him or herself switching instinctively between styles according to the people and work they are dealing with. This is referred to as **situational leadership** or **contingency theory**.

In an emergency for example, where a quick decision is needed, it can be absolutely right to take an autocratic approach. If on the other hand, you are trying to solve a customer problem with a competent team of people, you are likely to get better results through participation.

Analysts have found effective leadership to be contingent on a number of factors including:

◆ the work involved; whether it is routine or new and creative

◆ the organisational environment; whether it is stable or radically changing, conservative or adventurous

◆ your own preferred or natural style

◆ the skill levels, motivation and confidence of the team members you are working with.

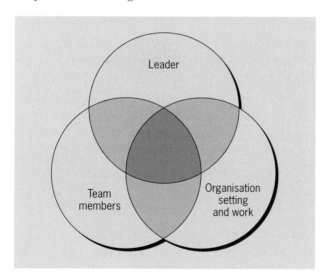

Figure 1.6 *Influences on leadership*

Leadership and relationships

What is it that makes people follow a leader? Another way to think about leadership is to look at the relationship between leader and followers. According to Bennis (1992), people will follow their leader if they meet some of their pivotal needs:

> **Too many leaders act as if the sheep.. their people.. are there for the benefit of the shepherd, not that the shepherd has responsibility for the sheep.**

To meet people's needs for:	Leaders should provide:	This will create:
Meaning and direction	Sense of purpose	Vision and goals
Trust	'Hardiness' (confidence that things will work out)	Energy and commitment
Hope and optimism	Authentic relationships	Reliability and consistency
Results	Bias toward action, risk, curiosity, and courage	Confidence and creativity

Table 1.4 *Serving the needs of followers*

Experts distinguish between two types of leadership: transactional and transformational.

Transactional leaders forge a trade-off with their followers (if you do this, then I will...), using rewards and punishment to encourage them to co-operate. They enable their followers to act in their own self-interest, as long as the leaders achieve their goals. In other words, leader and followers exchange needs and services to meet their independent objectives. It is an effective way to manage the status quo in an environment that is essentially stable, but it does not necessarily maximise follower potential.

Transformational leaders on the other hand focus more on creating a vision for change. Importantly, the vision needs to reflect the values and aspirations that leaders share with their followers. There is a common sense of purpose which is so powerful that it encourages followers to forget self-interest and to move toward fulfilling greater ideals. The vision acts as a powerful motivator encouraging followers to focus on key goals and to align individual efforts. With the vision in place, transformational leaders are able to delegate responsibility and to maximise the confidence, creativity and energy within their team.

Activity 3
Approaches to leadership

Objective

In this activity, you draw together your learning from this first theme to assess how you maximise your talents as a leader.

Task

1. What would you say are your strengths as a leader? Build on the work that you did in Activities 1 and 2.

2. Now think of two different people that you work with in a leadership role. To what extent do you adapt your leadership style to each personality? Is your approach effective?

3. What other factors affect your leadership style?

4. When you are leading a team, how do you meet peoples' needs for meaning and direction, trust, hope and optimism and results?

To meet people's needs for:	I do this by:
Meaning and direction	
Trust	
Hope and optimism	
Results	

5. What should you do more of? What should you do less of?

Feedback

Most managers will say they want to be a successful leader but few have actually worked out what success means to them. Taking some time out to visualise the type of leader you would like to be will help you target your leadership learning and to create some clear goals and plans.

While leaders report much valuable learning from courses and books, it is learning on the job which seems to provide the richest experience. The nature of the organisation – its norms, structure and culture – has an enormous bearing on the success of the leader. We look in the next theme at the dynamics of organisations and explore the relationship between organisational structure, culture and leadership.

◆ Recap

Explore the relationship between leadership and management in contemporary organisations

◆ Management is about coping with complexity. It brings a degree of order and consistency to key dimensions like the quality and profitability of products. Leadership, by contrast, is about relationships and influencing and is fundamental to change.

◆ Leadership has been the subject of extensive research and there are a variety of theories from which you can draw inspiration for your development. These include:

Trait theories are based on the idea that certain qualities or personality traits are important for leadership. Honesty, forward looking, competent and integrity are examples.

Behavioural frameworks identify what good leaders do in key skills areas such as communication, motivation and decision making. They are useful for benchmarking your performance.

Contingency theories focus on the situational factors that affect leadership. They suggest that leaders need to be able to practice a range of leadership styles and to adapt their style to meet the needs of their followers and the situations.

Transformational theories are to do with winning the hearts and minds of people through the creation of a shared vision, so generating not just compliance but energetic commitment.

Table 1.5 *Models of leadership*

Identify the diverse roles of the modern manager and explore your strengths and preferences

◆ Quinn argues that the 'managerial leader' needs to be able to play a number of roles; innovator, broker, producer, director, co-ordinator, monitor, facilitator and mentor.

◆ Your beliefs about what constitutes a good manager, coupled with your own natural strengths mean that you are likely to place more emphasis on and be better at some roles than others. Quinn cautions becoming trapped in a particular style of working and suggest that managers need to develop their competence across all eight roles.

Explore why leaders need to be self-aware and practice techniques to develop self-awareness

◆ By continuously developing your self-awareness you can gain more control over your behaviour and enhance your understanding of others. This in turn can improve the way you work with people, for example when coaching, giving feedback, reviewing performance and resolving problems.

◆ Two techniques that you can make use of to become more self-aware include:

   – reflection

   – feedback

 **More @**

Hersey, P. and Blanchard, K. H (1999) *Leadership and the One Minute Manager*, **William Morrow**
A slim and easy to access guide to situational leadership.

Mintzberg, H. (1990) *Mintzberg on Management: Inside our strange world of organisations*, **New York, The Free Press**
Mintzberg offers a different framework for management development as does the website which sets out the national management standards in the UK.
(www.management-standards.org)

Northouse, P. G. (2004) *Leadership: Theory and Practice*, **Sage Publications, Inc.**
For more on leadership theory and how it can inform practice, this is a useful book.

Quinn, R., Faerman, S., Thompson, M. and McGrath, M. (2002), *Becoming a Master Manager*, **Wiley**
Focused around the Competing Values Framework introduced at the start of this theme, *Becoming a Master Manager*, provides more detail and development activities for each of the competences.

www.mindtools.com and www.leadertoleader.org are websites that offer access to an excellent range of skills development resources and opinion pieces to support your work in this book.

2   The organisational setting

> 'Effective leadership can't easily be separated from an organisation and its mission. The nature of the organisation – its norms, cultures and processes – make up the stage on which the leadership drama is played, and that stage has a large bearing on the success of the leader.'

Zenger (2000)

It is often claimed that the organisational setting dictates far more about what leadership style will be best than any other variable. Take skilful leaders on the football field for example. To achieve similar success in a research institution, they would need to adapt their style considerably.

In this section we focus on two essential aspects of the organisational setting: structure and culture. As a manager you might not be able to change the structure or culture of your organisation, but you need to understand its dynamics. First these give you an essential insight into decision making processes and second, they help you plan how to maximise performance, both your own and the performance of your team.

You will:

◆ explore why organisational structure and culture need to be aligned if an organisation is to achieve its strategic goals

◆ review how organisational structures are changing to enable organisations to become more agile and responsive to their stakeholders

◆ explore how organisations can influence the development of a high performance culture as a source of competitive advantage

◆ evaluate the culture of your organisation and team and assess what this means for effective management practice.

Organisations – structure and culture in balance

Organisations can be small, involving a few people in one location, or they can be extremely complex. They can be self-contained such as a private company, a public body such as a local authority, a not-for-profit organisation, or an autonomous operating unit within a larger organisation. Organisations can be defined in terms of the sectors they serve or the products and services they offer. Microsoft and Tesco both provide us with products but are vastly different in what they do.

When any group of people work together to achieve specific goals, the context in which they work could be called an organisation. What separates organisations from other activities is that organisations usually operate within a defined structure.

The formal organisation

All organisations are structured in some way. When a small consultancy hires an administrator to deal with the paperwork, they are in fact designing a structure albeit an informal one. In reality, small organisations have little need for standardisation of jobs or for formal structure – when a job needs to be done, people share the work – and they are able to remain informal with respect to roles, rules and procedures.

In larger organisations however there would be chaos without some level of organisation. Larger organisations depend for their longer term success on their ability to determine the tasks to be done, who will do them, and how those tasks will be managed and co-ordinated. Take a look at the following organisation chart or use the one for your organisation. What does it tell you about the organisation?

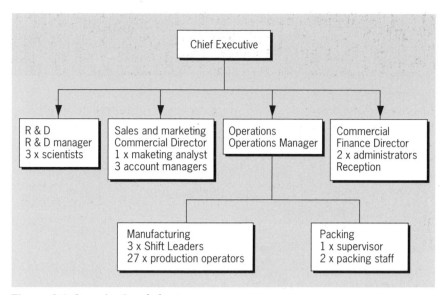

Figure 2.1 *Organisational chart*

The structure gives us an insight into where power and authority lie in the organisation and about how decisions get made. Key features of the structure include:

◆ **Vertical hierarchy**. Some organisations will have many levels whereas others manage to operate with relatively few. Communication tends to be more effective in flatter organisations because there are less layers for the message to pass through. Similarly decision making can be quicker.

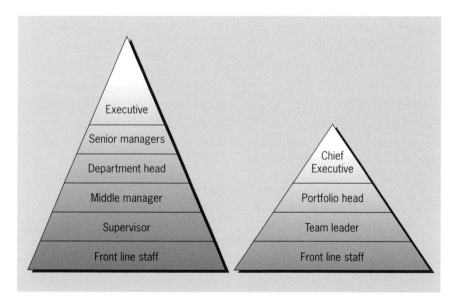

Figure 2.2 *Vertical complexity*

◆ **Span of control**. Span of control relates to the number of people who report to a single manager. Span of control and hierarchy are closely related. Where there are fewer layers of management, managers typically have wider spans of control and vice versa. A wider span of control encourages managers to share power and delegate work effectively. It can, however, be challenging in a team that is inexperienced.

◆ **Functional and geographical groupings.** The 'boxes' at a horizontal level on the chart show whether jobs and departments are grouped by function, by geography, by product or some other means again. The way in which work is organised between departments and teams affects organisational efficiency and effectiveness and is something we look at later in this theme.

The organisation chart depicts what is known as the 'formal' organisation. The formal organisation refers essentially to the rules and structures that the organisation puts in place so that people can carry out their jobs. It includes for example job descriptions, rewards, communication processes, reporting lines etc...

The informal organisation

In most organisations there is also an informal way of working. This is called the organisational culture or the 'way things get done around here'. The culture is less obvious than the formal structure but it has an enormous impact on the way people behave.

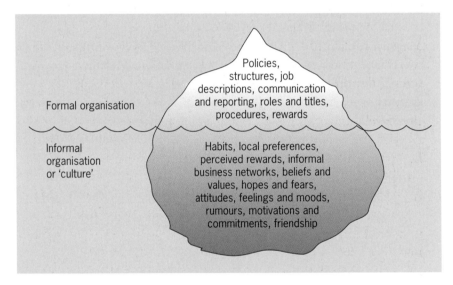

Figure 2.3 *The organisational iceberg*   *Source: (adapted from Plant (1987)*

The concept of organisational culture has attracted a good deal of research over the past 20 years, especially associated with workplace attitudes and performance. The core idea is that every organisation has a set of shared assumptions and values about business, working life and relationships. These values influence the way people behave towards each other and towards customers, and how they relate to their work.

> **A company is known by the people it keeps.**
> **Anonymous**

You can gain a feel for an organisation's culture through your first impressions. How the staff deal with you. What the physical surroundings are like. The type of behaviour they expect from you. These are all indications of the culture and will vary from one organisation to the next. Read through the case scenarios below for Omega Holdings and Uberspace Labs. If you could work for one of them, which would it be and why?

Uberspace Labs

Janine is a marketing analyst at Uberspace Labs, an innovative satellite firm on a science park near Cambridge. Although she typically works 45 hours a week, her schedule is extremely flexible and can vary according to her responsibilities toward her son. The thing Janine loves about her job is that she can come and go as she is needed; some days she comes in very early in the morning, and other days she might not come into until late in the afternoon. Dress is extremely casual, as it most everything at Uberspace Labs. It's not unusual for people to drop into other people's offices, even the Chief Executive's without appointment. The lines of communication are very informal but somehow everyone seems to know what is going on and is keen to play their part.

Omega Holdings

Sami loosens his tie behind his office door hoping that no-one will knock for a while so he can relax. Omega Holdings has a strict dress code requiring suits with ties for men, heels for women and no exceptions. They are a slick City based operation pricing themselves in the upper quartile of consultancies. Goals are very clear, rules are respected and it is not unusual for people to receive a low performance evaluation for being late once or twice in a six-month period. It took Sami a while to adjust when he joined. His first task had been to undertake a competitor analysis and he had mentioned in a fairly off-hand way that he'd be able to deliver a snapshot report in a 'week or so'. Now in his previous company, 'a week or so' could mean anything up to a month, sometimes longer. So four days later when his manager asked his for his report, Sami was surprised. When he asked why he wanted it so quickly, his manager levelled a particularly formidable gaze at him and said 'Because you said so'. He left Sami in no doubt that unless he delivered a high-quality report on time, he might as well start looking for a new contract. When after a couple of months, Sami offered his ideas for improving sales to the Sales Director, he was told that he should make his suggestions through his immediate superior. The communication lines at Omega Holdings are very formal.

Omega Holdings and Uberspace Labs are two very different organisations with very different cultures – one has very relaxed rules and other very rigid rules. One has very open communication while the other doesn't. If you are the kind of person who doesn't likes rules, enjoys informality and can tolerate ambiguity, then Uberspace Labs may be the place for you. However, if you like clear policies and a more formal working situation then you might be more comfortable at Omega Holdings.

What's important to understand is that neither company is better off than the other in terms of its success. In fact those who work for the two companies are likely to be happy with their jobs and with the company. Schein (1988) describes culture as the shared assumptions and values that shape member's behaviours. So if you share the values of the organisation that you work for, you are likely to be happy to work there with the converse being true as well.

To start to unpack the culture of your organisation, try asking:

◆ How do decisions get made? Is decision making formal or informal?

◆ What do people pay attention to? For example, if decisions are always made on the basis of cost, then you probably work in a cost rather than a customer driven culture.

◆ Is status and hierarchy important or is there a feeling that all people are equal? Do people have their own offices or is it open-plan? Are there reserved parking spaces?

◆ What types of behaviour is the norm? Do people listen to each other or shoot each other down in meetings. Is it a competitive or a supportive culture?

◆ What happens when people make mistakes? Is it treated as a learning opportunity or is there a culture of allocating blame?

> **Redrawing the lines and boxes in your org chart without addressing the way people within the organisation interact may be like rearranging the deck chairs on the Titanic.**
> **Peter Senge**

Structure and culture in balance

Research suggests that organisations are most effective in achieving their objectives when their structure and culture are in balance. Nadler and Tushman (1997) identify structure and culture as two of the key building blocks that an organisation must align as it pursues its strategy.

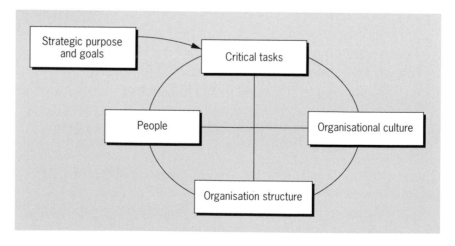

Figure 2.4 *Organisational congruence*

Source: adapted from Nadler and Tushman (1997)

- Critical tasks – work processes that need to be in place and critical tasks that need to be completed.

- Formal organisational structure and process – roles, rewards and incentives, decision making structure (centralised versus decentralised), departmental structures, work processes etc…

- People – competencies and capabilities and the HR policies that relate to recruitment, selection and development of people in order to create the necessary talent pool.

- Culture – norms, values, communication networks, informal roles and power that people hold.

An example here would be Marks & Spencer. Before it hit its trading difficulties in the nineties, their structure was highly complex with many layers of management. Their culture was renowned for a high level of loyalty, lifetime employment and a paternalistic management style. For a long time this was successful. Their culture and structure were in balance and the market was stable.

However when the business environment changes, as it did for Marks & Spencer, through increased competition, economic downturn or whatever, organisations are forced to change with it. Often the response is to develop a new competitive strategy and to re-organise. But without an equal shift in culture, and the development of people and new work processes, the organisation will find itself out of alignment and with significant barriers to change.

Activity 4
Organisational congruence

Objective

In this activity, you explore the issues in aligning the four building blocks of critical tasks, people, culture and structure with company strategy.

Task

1. You have recently been appointed as a strategic consultant to Wildings.

A NEW WAY FOR WILDINGS

An icon of UK business shattered on Monday when department store chain, Wildings. said it would close 17 retail stores, eliminate 2000 jobs, and stop publishing the legendary Wildings catalogue, which has since the war brought quality home and gardenware into UK homes.

Wildings enjoyed its number one status in the UK retailing business until a flawed diversification strategy led it to venture into several unrelated areas and to lose focus. The retailing major failed to sense the changing trend in selling and merchandising. Competition from the internet, supermarkets and discount stores, coupled with a lazy and arrogant response by their own management, has now forced a retreat to the company's core retail business. Analysts predict that the business is ripe for a takeover, but new CEO, Dave Goldman has other ideas.

2. Dave Goleman and his board have drawn up an aggressive vision and identified the critical tasks required to become competitive. They have brought you in to carry out a capability audit in relation to the organisation structure, culture and its people. Your audit highlights that major changes are required. The key points from your analysis are set out below.

   What changes will you recommend to the new CEO to bring the organisation back into alignment?

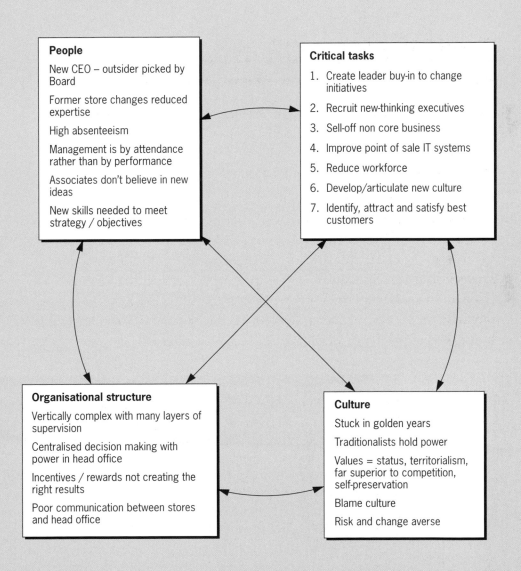

Strategic business and goals

1. Focus on core business
2. Make Wildings a more compelling place to shop
3. Increase local market forces
4. Improve cost structure and profitability

Vision:

Regain leadership in the retail industry

People

New CEO – outsider picked by Board

Former store changes reduced expertise

High absenteeism

Management is by attendance rather than by performance

Associates don't believe in new ideas

New skills needed to meet strategy / objectives

Critical tasks

1. Create leader buy-in to change initiatives
2. Recruit new-thinking executives
3. Sell-off non core business
4. Improve point of sale IT systems
5. Reduce workforce
6. Develop/articulate new culture
7. Identify, attract and satisfy best customers

Organisational structure

Vertically complex with many layers of supervision

Centralised decision making with power in head office

Incentives / rewards not creating the right results

Poor communication between stores and head office

Culture

Stuck in golden years

Traditionalists hold power

Values = status, territorialism, far superior to competition, self-preservation

Blame culture

Risk and change averse

Figure 2.5 *Organisational congruence at Wildings*

Feedback

Wildings needs to consider each of the building blocks if it is to survive and be competitive. You might have started by looking at the structure. Removing layers of hierarchy and decentralising some of the decision making would improve the flexibility of the organisation and its ability to respond to customers. Setting productivity goals and new reward structures would help to build momentum for change.

On its own however, this would not be enough. The Wildings culture would not be able to support the new competitive strategy and structure, nor do its people have the skills that are required. New behaviours will be required including:

◆ freedom to make decisions without a long approval process

◆ teamwork between stores and head office

◆ people become more accountable and less inclined to blame others

◆ openness to new ideas particularly cost-effectiveness

◆ a willingness to take risks.

To achieve this, Wildings needs to embark on a culture change programme that includes training and development for its people who lack the skills and attitudes that will be essential for change.

Designing organisational structures and culture change programmes are challenging areas and in the rest of this theme, we introduce some of the key concepts.

Organisational structures – from hierarchies to network organisations

We start with structure. An effective organisational structure will facilitate working relationships between various sections of the organisation and will retain order and command while promoting flexibility and creativity. As the oldest form of structure, the hierarchy is probably the most familiar, but matrix and network structures are becoming increasingly common as organisations seek to enhance their ability to respond rapidly to their changing business environment.

Functional organisations: Enhancing operational efficiency

One of the most common forms of hierarchy is the functional structure. This is often the first structure that an organisation evolves as it starts to grow.

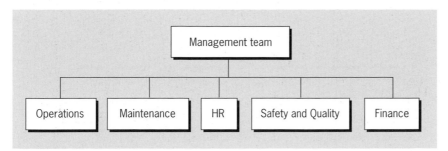

Figure 2.6 *The functional organisation*

Functional organisations are simple to understand with clear lines of command, well defined tasks and responsibilities. By grouping staff with similar skills, the organisation promotes functional excellence and can achieve economies of scale through specialisation. On the flip side though, these functional groups can become so cohesive that they develop a silo mentality with people showing a greater commitment to their function than to the organisation. This can render the organisation slow to respond to interfunctional problems and to the needs of the end user client.

Divisional structures: Providing focus

As organisations grow they are likely to adopt a divisional structure. Structuring the organisation by division creates a number of departments based for example on the organisation's products, services, clients or the geographical territories in which it operates.

Product or service	An insurance company might group people to focus on pensions, home insurance and the various products that are delivered to customers
Geography or territory	A retail chain or similar business where the service or product needs to be delivered locally might adopt this structure
Client	A telecommunications business might be structured into consumer and business divisions

Table 2.1 *Grouping by division*

Organising by division increases efficiency because the departments can become more responsive to the needs of clients within a particular segment or geography. Less favourably, there is often duplication of effort and it can be more difficult for people doing similar sorts of work to share ideas, learn from each other and achieve economies of scale.

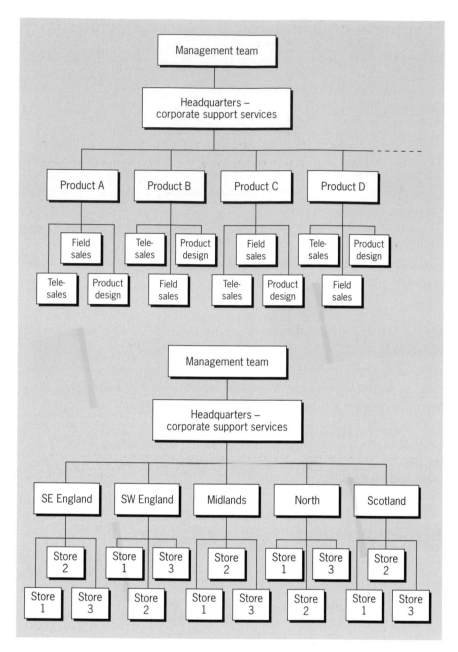

Figure 2.7 *The divisional organisation*

Matrix structures: Providing a dual focus

Matrix organisations seek to loosen up some of the bureaucracies and rigidities associated with hierarchies. In matrix organisations, employees are assigned to:

1. a functional area which provides a stable base for specialised activities and a permanent base for members of staff

2. cross functional project teams that integrate the activities of functional departments by focusing on specific products or territories for example.

In this example, from a management training company, staff from different functional areas work together in project teams formed around product areas. The matrix structure establishes a grid, or matrix, in which two lines of authority work together to make a balanced decision. Authority and responsibility flows down through the line management function and horizontally through project teams where authority and responsibility is delegated through a project manager.

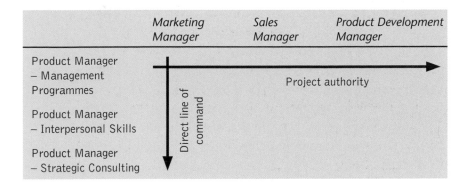

Figure 2.8 *The matrix organisation*

Within a matrix, no one person has sole decision making power over a particular situation or particular type of decision. This breaks down the traditional hierarchies that characterise both functional and divisional organisations and creates a structure in which it is possible for people to be more readily empowered.

Benefits	Considerations
◆ Greater flexibility to adapt to specific strategic situations	◆ Complex leading to slow decision making
◆ Can achieve simultaneous objectives	◆ Reporting to two bosses can cause ambiguity and conflict, leading to stress and preference for one above the other
◆ Promotes knowledge sharing and learning across the organisation	
◆ Leaves functional managers free to concentrate on developing and deploying staff members	◆ Functional groups may neglect their normal duties and responsibilities
◆ Dedicated project managers focus on completion of mission-critical projects	◆ Difficulty for project managers in defining extent of authority over staff from functional departments

Table 2.2 Benefits and considerations of a matrix structure

Network structures: the key to flexibility

A more recent organisational form to emerge is the Managed Network.

> In the spring of 1999, a group of Marines stormed the beaches of Northern California in an exercise called 'Urban Warrior,' where they tested combat tactics, new technologies, and a different way of organizing – one that diverges from their traditional command-and-control, top-down structure. The Marines realise that in an environment characterised by uncertainty, a rigid, hierarchical organisational structure can inhibit important characteristics such as flexibility and adaptability. For the Marines, this uncertain environment stems from the complexities of new threats to national security – warlords in Mogadishu, separatists in Kosovo, thugs in Haiti.
>
> The Marines are calling their new approach 'networkcentric warfare,' and it involves rethinking the fundamental ways in which they have worked for over 200 years. Network-centric warfare refers not only to an electronic network – new communication technologies are connecting Marines through satellites and LAN systems – but also refers to how Marines define the way they organise on the battlefield. Through exercises like 'Urban Warrior,' the Marines want to find out if they can transform themselves into a human network – a structure that many believe to be more adaptive and flexible than a traditional hierarchy.

Source: www.leader-values.com

Like the Marines, some corporations are trying to become more adaptive to the needs of their stakeholders by adopting more flexible structures known as Managed Networks.

The aim is a loosely coupled network that is guided through a central hub and lateral relationships rather than by a hierarchical chain of command. Such a network might exist within an organisation or involve alliances with other organisations.

The key benefit of a network is that it is exceptionally agile so it can excel at a local level. 'Specialisation' is a key word because:

◆ each unit will have its own specialism making it more likely to recognise and correctly interpret impending environmental shifts that affect their areas of expertise

◆ groups of specialists operating together are more likely to craft creative solutions.

While there is no disputing these benefits, the challenge in a Managed Network is to add some degree of structure and management without destroying the very qualities that make them effective. Networks are notoriously difficult to manage. Semco SA, the Brazilian machinery manufacturer that you look at in Activity 5 below, is essentially a network.

Choosing the right structure

What matters is that the structure that is chosen facilitates the organisation in achieving its purpose and the needs of the organisation's stakeholders. Lynch (2003) provides some useful examples of the implications that an organisation's purpose and its activities might have on its structure:

Purpose	Implications for organisation structure
'Ideas factory' such as an advertising or promotions agency	Loose, fluid structure able to respond rapidly to its customers. As it grows in size, however more formal structures are usually inevitable.
Local authority or civil service department	Strict controls on procedures and authorisations. Strong formal structures to handle major policy directions and legal issues.
Non-profit making charity with a strong sense of mission	Reliance on voluntary members and their voluntary contributions may require a flexible organisation with responsibility devolved to individuals.
Multinational company in branded goods	Major linkage and resource issues that need carefully co-ordinated structures e.g. on common suppliers or common supermarket customers for separate product ranges.
Major service company such as a retail bank or electricity generating company	Formal structures but supported by some flexibility so that variations in demand can be met quickly.
Small business attempting to survive and grow	Informal willingness to undertake several business functions such as selling and production depending on the short-term circumstances.
Health service with strong professional service ethics, standards and quality	Formalised structure that reflects the seniority and professional status of those involved while delivering the crucial complex service provisions.

Table 2.3 *Organisational purpose and structure*   Source: Lynch (2003)

Activity 5
An unusual workplace

Objective

Semco is probably one of the best known Network Organisations shaped through the maverick and revolutionary beliefs of its CEO Richard Semler. In this activity, you explore Semler's approach to leadership.

> Executives must give up control and trust the power of talent. Only then will that person's calling emerge.

Richard Semler (1993)

Task

1. Read through the case study below:

Semco posted a 2005 turnover of well over US$200 million. It has no official structure and no head office. If people want a desk they go online and reserve space at one of the few satellite offices in São Paulo. There are no job titles, job descriptions or employee contracts. The company rotates leadership positions including the CEO.

There's no business plan or mission statement. There is no chief officer for information technology; people are encouraged to select the IT that they need. There is no human resources department and no career plans. There are no time clocks, dress codes or perks for top executives.

Semco has undergone a radical transformation from the paternalistic hierarchy that Semler inherited from his father in the early 80s. At the core of the transformation is Semler's firm belief that all people desire to achieve excellence.

In 'Maverick, the success behind the world's most unusual workforce', he tells how in the late 1980s, three Semco engineers submitted a proposal to take a small group of employees 'raised in Semco's culture and set them free.' The stated aim of the group was to invent and reinvent new products, refine marketing strategies and dream up new lines of business. Twice a year they proposed to report to senior management at which time their mandate would be extended for another six months or revoked. Semler true to his belief in democratic autonomous teams approved the proposal.

At the end of the first six months, the Nucleus of Technological Innovation (NTI) team had eighteen projects in progress. Its success was to set the foundation for a model for change at Semco. In 1990 Semler and his senior managers decided to encourage the creative and entrepreneurial spirit of employees by encouraging the creation of more satellites like NTI through the organisation. As an added incentive to foster growth, Semler guaranteed initial contract work for the new satellites. Satellite businesses turned out to be among the most innovative and agile divisions within Semco. Today roughly two thirds of Semco's products come from satellite companies.

Semler has said that he tried to reconstruct the company so that Semco could govern itself on the basis of three values: employee participation, profit sharing, and open information systems. Participation gives people control of their work, profit sharing gives them a reason to do it better, information tells them what's working and what isn't.

Many workers, including factory workers, set their own schedules. They can also choose their own form of compensation based on 11 different options. What prevents associates from taking advantage of this freedom? First, all the company's financial information is public, so everyone knows what everyone else earns. People who pay themselves too much have to work with resentful colleagues. Not long ago, union members argued that their pay increase was too high and would hurt profitability. Second, all associates must reapply for their jobs every six months and must secure the support of fellow associates to be successful. Pay yourself unfairly, and you could soon be looking for a new job.

Collective decision-making is down to a fine art at Semco. For example, worker committees run the manufacturing plants and profit-sharing schemes are available to all staff members. Employees can, with a show of hands, veto new product ideas or scrap whole business ventures.

Semler asserts that not controlling is so difficult for people in senior positions that this gives Semco its competitive advantage. 'If you don't know where people are, you can't possibly key an eye of them. All that's left to judge on is performance.'

Source: Adapted from (2006) and (1993)

1. What are the key features of the Semco organisation that has enabled it to achieve its success?

2. Many managers would be uncomfortable with the lack of structure and the level of employee participation at Semco. What is your view?

Feedback

1. The lack of formal structure at Semco might sound like a recipe for chaos and anarchy but it has been a key feature in fostering an entrepreneurial culture. Semco has business operations as diverse as manufacturing industrial machinery and mixers for pharmaceutical and candy companies, builds cooling towers, runs office buildings' data centers and provides consulting services on environmental issues.

   Semler's conviction that employees who participate in important decisions would naturally be more highly motivated and make better choices than those who simply followed orders from above has been pivotal in his success. His whole business philosophy is based on giving freedom to his staff and inspiring them to assume ownership and responsibility. His words and actions (enabling people to set their own salaries, make their own decisions) constantly say, 'I trust you, I believe in you, and you are an integral part of this company's success.'

   Obviously the chance to contribute in a meaningful way gives people a sense of accomplishment and self-realisation. More subtle however is the bond that participation creates between employees and their peers. As employees work more closely, they begin to feel solidarity with each other. This relationship gives each employee a very personal stake in the success of teamwork. Social pressures to pull your weight become a powerful source of motivation and in the Semco model they take the place of executive, top-down control.

   Associates have to reapply for their jobs every six months. Says Semler, 'The system is pretty unforgiving, because if you put your salary too high, and people don't put you on the list as someone they need for the next six months, you're in trouble.' Workers select and rate their bosses and the information is made public.

2. Semco might be an extreme example of participative decision making, but as a concept the approach is very topical. Many organisations are grappling with how to move from a culture where decision-making is centralised to one that is more participative. The approach needs to be led. Many managers would be uncomfortable with sacrificing their authority to the extent advocated by Semler. Managers need to decide exactly what they are trying to achieve by increasing participation before establishing relevant levels. If the objective for example, is solely to reduce employee resistance then participation should be set at a more limited level than if you are trying to unleash greater creative potential of the workforce. We look in some detail at empowerment and the extent to which it is realistic to empower staff in the final theme of this book.

What kind of organisational culture do you have?

One of the biggest challenges in trying to understand your own culture is that it is difficult for someone on the inside to see. Edgar Schein (2004) describes culture as:

> A pattern of shared basic assumptions that the group learned as it solved its problems of external adaptation and internal integration, that has worked well enough to be considered valid and, therefore, to be taught to new members as the correct way you perceive, think, and feel in relation to those problems.

The team at Semco (Activity 5) was driven by a conviction that highly participative decision-making would result in more motivated staff, and as this proved true, so the conviction became more and more deeply held. Now Semco no longer questions the approach, participation is assumed to be the way to go. To act in any other way would violate what is now a core value.

If organisation structure and design is the skeleton and muscles of the organisation, organisational culture is the organisation's spirit or soul.
Anon

It is possible to unpack the culture that drives your own organisation through analysis. Schein provides us with a model which views culture at three levels:

Figure 2.9 *Schein's three levels of culture*

Artefacts are visible

At the topmost level are artefacts. Although the values and beliefs that drive culture might be invisible, artefacts are not. These are the visible things that the company does to explain its culture and to send messages to new people about how to behave.

> **Get big fast**
>
> In Amazon.com's formative years CEO Jeff Bezos, repeatedly reminded employees that customers didn't care what the offices or desks looked like. His own desk he made out of an exterior door and some angle brackets. All the other furniture was purchased used from garage sales or auctions.
>
> 'We have a strong focus on trying to spend money on things that matter to customers and not spend money on us', said Bezos.

Source: Spector (2000)

Artefacts take a number of forms:

◆ Stories that people tell about the organisation and its culture. These often reflect basic themes such as whether the organisational culture supports equality or inequality, control or lack of control, work-life balance or a long hours culture.

◆ Symbols that stand for or suggest something else. For example impressive offices and job titles suggest status, dress codes suggest the level of formality, pictures of organisational successes on the wall suggest achievement.

- Heroes are company role models. Through their performance they highlight the values the company wishes to reinforce. Heroes are often the main characters in organisational stories.

- Rituals that guide behaviour in daily organisational life including such things as how associates greet one another, how visitors are met, who makes the coffee, dress down days and ceremonies like employee of the month.

Values bind people together

At the middle level of Schein's model are values. These are the things we say about ourselves.

- We are committed to improvement

- We value customers

- We believe that work should be fun

Try looking on the websites of some of the larger organisations for their values. Also try looking at some public sector and non-profit organisations like universities, local government, Red Cross and Greenpeace. Ask yourself what purpose these statements serve and for whom?

Some companies such as Semco see their values (employee participation, open information, profit sharing) as a source of competitive advantage. But for values to have this kind of impact, they must form the bedrock of organisational culture. When a set of values is truly shared, employees are committed to behaving in a certain way; they know which actions are considered acceptable or unacceptable. Shared values have a powerful effect on the norms and standards within an organisation, from the way the organisation deals with its customers to the way it treats its staff.

> Values are like fingerprints. Nobody's are the same, but you leave 'em all over everything you do,
> **Elvis Presley**

Underlying assumptions

Digging deeper, the third layer of culture is 'underlying assumptions'. Assumptions are the taken for granted beliefs, perceptions and feelings which we have developed over time. It is these that are at the root of culture and that you need to dig for to unearth the real assumptions that are driving performance in your organisation.

Influencing culture

There are significant benefits to developing a strong culture, where firstly there is a clear set of values and beliefs and secondly these are widely shared among organisational members.

Kelleher, CEO, says that culture is the source of competitive advantage at Southwest airlines. Kelleher acknowledges that Southwest does a lot right. They use point-to-point routes, fly relatively new planes, use only one type of plane, and are famous for 'no frills' – no meals and no assigned seats. When asked in a taped interview why he doesn't consider those things the reason for competitive advantage, Kelleher's says ardently, 'All those things could be copied by a competitor tomorrow. The only thing they can't copy is our culture.'

Source: Turknett and Hitchcock (1998)

In recent years many organisations have started to recognise the power of shared values and beliefs in guiding behaviour and have articulated what they believe their core values are or should be. Here is an example from the Body Shop:

Body Shop mission statement

◆ To dedicate our business to the pursuit of social and environmental change.

◆ To creatively balance the financial and human needs of our stakeholders: employees, customers, franchisees, suppliers and shareholders.

◆ To courageously ensure that our business is ecologically sustainable: meeting the needs of the present without compromising the future.

◆ To meaningfully contribute to local, national and international communities in which we trade, by adopting a code of conduct which ensures care, honesty, fairness and respect.

◆ To passionately campaign for the protection of the environment, human and civil rights, and against animal testing within the cosmetics and toiletries industry.

◆ To tirelessly work to narrow the gap between principle and practice, whilst making fun, passions and care part of our daily lives.

Source: www.bodyshop.co.uk

Culture change experts, Senn Delaney Leadership (2000) note that while all organisations develop their own unique culture, there are four core values that seem to underpin all high performance cultures:

◆ Ethics and integrity

◆ Openness and trust; embracing change

◆ Accountability and empowerment (making it happen)

◆ Teamwork.

You can probably think of other important values which may be subsets or additions to these. Quality, service and customer-focus, innovation and diversity are all important guiding behaviours.

The management challenge lies not just in deciding the values but in making them a way of life. How managers (and in particular senior managers) behave is the single most important factor in meeting this challenge. Think for a moment about how you could instigate a can-do culture or a learning culture or, less desirably, a blame culture in your team.

> **Our job is to provide a culture in which people can flourish and reach their dreams – in which they can be all they want to be.**
> **Jack Welch**

What you as a manager do shapes the 'way things get done' in your team. To encourage a can-do culture you'd have to enable team members to take on responsibilities and to support them. A learning culture would involve encouraging the team to get into the habit of reviewing what has happened and learn from it. To get a blame culture you just need to make sure that anyone who admits to a mistake gets criticised, ridiculed or disciplined. People will soon catch on and start blaming everyone else.

Managers need to act as exemplary models, and where they do not, they effectively give permission to others to do the same. Research indicates that leadership organisations use a mix of methods to embed their core values:

- Communication through mottos, mission and vision statements. The informal motto of 'Do no evil' adopted by Google when it went public is an example of a highly visible values-led management approach.

- Consistency is also crucial. Saying empowerment is a value and then holding onto information will not work. Google came up against intense criticism that jeapordised the impact of the 'Do no evil' slogan when, to gain access to the Chinese market, it censored its search engine.

- Enthusiasm and passion. Don't let the message get boring.

- Reinforcing the desired culture with symbols and other artifacts. If the objective of the culture change is teamwork, then changing the office layout to open plan sends the right message.

- Training and coaching. Shaping a culture requires feedback and support, firstly to help people find meaning in the new values and then to help them develop their behavioural style.

Changing culture is not easy. According to Senn Delaney it requires an almost obsessive attention to detail. 'If we are to change a culture, we must become acutely aware of what we do and the message it communicates. We must get off automatic pilot.'

Activity 6
The culture in your organisation

Objective

In this activity we ask you to think about the values, beliefs and culture of your organisation and to identify examples of how these drive your behaviour.

Task

1. What would you say are the core values that drive behaviour in your organisation? Select one or two of these and think of examples when they have affected your behaviour as a manager. To what extent do you share the core values of your organisation?

2. How do you as a manager build commitment amongst the team to your organisation's values?

Feedback

1. The level of congruence or match between an organisation's values and those of its staff has important outcomes for the individual and for the organisation. Congruence between organisational and employee values is linked significantly with organisational commitment and the sense of obligation that employees feel towards their company. In other words you are likely to be happier if you share the values of the organisation for which you work with the converse being true as well.

2. Managers play a key role as communicators of values. Firstly as a role model but secondly in helping to make values real and accessible to the people in your team. Take advantage of opportunities through feedback to highlight where someone has displayed a core value or where their performance could be improved. Use stories and examples to help illustrate what the value means in your work area and why they are important to the business.

Managing subcultures

So far in this theme we have talked about organisational culture as a single entity. In fact within any one organisation there are likely to be several subcultures. These may be made up of people who work together in a team, work in a specific location, share the same racial background or the same professional occupation.

An important point to recognise is that the more diverse the subcultures are within an organisation, the wider the range of self interests that are likely to exist. Consider the following:

> **Principal:** ' My college espouses values of inclusion; we try to make sure that all students are given the best possible support in their transition to adulthood and we bend over backwards to try and make sure that students are given every chance to succeed. We treat everyone the same.'
>
> **Lecturer:** 'I do not see why I should put up with disruptive pupils in my class. I have very large class sizes and it is just not possible to give each pupil individual attention. I think that disruptive and slow pupils are better off in a special school or unit so that the rest can get on with things.
>
> **Head of Pastoral Services:** 'In this college we all believe in the importance of the individual. We believe that each young person should be made to feel that they matter and that they are listened to.'
>
> **Caretaker:** 'There are some great kids in the school – but there are some real nuisances too. If we could just try to make sure that the nuisances were punished properly, maybe expel them from school, then my life and the teachers would be easier.'

It would be unrealistic and you might think undesirable to try and completely homogenise subcultures. It is healthy to have diversity of opinion. But you do need to recognise and manage situations when self-interest within a subculture, particularly within the area you manage, is in effect undermining the mission of the organisation as a whole.

Working across cultural boundaries

One of the biggest challenges that subcultures pose is the potential for conflict. To work effectively across cultural boundaries within an organisation, you need to be able to read the culture of those that you're dealing with and to see things from their perspective. You have to determine what behaviour is acceptable and unacceptable. What are the boundaries, norms and values of those you are trying to work with?

In Understanding Organisations, Charles Handy identifies four different cultural types which you can use to classify the culture or subcultures within your organisation.

Power culture

Control radiates from the centre

Power is concentrated in the hands of a few key people enabling the organisation or business area to move very quickly because decision-making is centralised. They often evolve in new businesses (or business units) which under the guidance of an entrepreneurial leader grow comparatively quickly, eventually becoming too big to be controlled by one or even a few people. The challenge then is for them to modify their culture and to spread power more effectively.

Role culture

Greek temples are sturdy structure built on solid ground.

People have very clear roles based on functions or expertise, e.g. the HR team or the Finance team. Effectiveness depends not so much on the quality of the individuals as it did in the power culture but on how rationally the work and responsibility are allocated. The role or the job is the most important factor. Control is through policies and procedures. Everyone has a designated job description, procedural handbook, hierarchical career path etc... Where economies of scale (consistency and quality) and specialisation are more important than flexibility or product innovation, a role culture is appropriate, but to be successful it requires a stable environment as role cultures are slow to change.

Task culture

Adaptable and egalitarian network

Accomplishment of the task rather than excellence within a role forms the emphasis. Teams with the right mix of expertise are brought together to solve particular problems. Organisations with a matrix structure have a task culture. Managers have the power to allocate projects and so maintain control but substantial power is delegated to team members. The mutual respect for each others expertise that develops within the group unites the work team as they pursue their goal. The task culture is very adaptable and so is relevant where flexibility is important. According to Handy it is, 'the culture most in tune with current ideologies of change and adaptation, individual freedom and low status differentials'.

Person culture

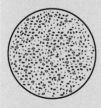

Galaxy of mixed stars

This is a less common culture. Its purpose is to serve the individual which would be difficult in most organisations where individuals need to pursue the organisational goals. Some professional partnerships can operate as person cultures, because each partner brings a peculiar expertise and clientele to the firm.

Table 2.4 *Culture types*

Activity 7
Working across cultural boundaries

Objective

Use this activity to think about the subcultures within your organisation and about how you as a manager can work effectively across cultural boundaries.

Task

1. Explain the culture in your team or business area using Handy's model. Is it a:

   ◆ power culture

   ◆ task culture

   ◆ role culture

   ◆ person culture

   How similar is it to other areas of the organisation that you work with?

2. How would you seek to influence decision making within a:

   ◆ power culture

   ◆ task culture

   ◆ role culture

   ◆ person culture

Feedback

Understanding the culture within your own organisation (or area of the organisation) and those you are dealing with can help you to adapt your strategies and behaviours so that you are effective. Understanding culture can also help you to more successfully gain influence.

In a power culture, for example, developing personal relationships and trust with the decision-makers matters far more than job title or position.

In a role culture this is not the case. Power comes from position and the easiest way to gain support is to make effective use of the rules and procedures. In a role culture, your position as manager will give you more influence than it would within a power or task culture.

In a task culture, the focus is strongly on achievement of the task and it is through showing how you support this that you can most easily gain influence. Your ability to provide expert input will be valuable.

A person culture differs again. The culture exists only to serve the interests of the people involved and you need to appeal to these if you are to gain influence.

We look in the next theme at influencing tools and techniques.

◆ Recap

Explore why organisational structure and culture need to be aligned if an organisation is to achieve its strategic goals.

◆ The structure and culture of an organisation need to be aligned and to support the strategies that the organisation and its stakeholders are seeking to achieve.

Review how organisational structures are changing to enable organisations to become more agile and responsive to their stakeholders.

◆ As organisations face pressure to become more and more responsive, they are moving away from bureaucracies and towards matrix structures that enable them to devolve decision making power to the front line. Network organisations are a newer and more flexible form of organisation. They are composed of specialist units that work in flexible configurations to meet stakeholder needs.

Explore how organisations can influence the development of a high performance culture as a source of competitive advantage.

◆ The culture – the way that things get done – of an organisation is shaped by the set of shared values and beliefs that bind its members together. Senn Delaney maintain that four values in particular are present at the core of high performance organisations:

 – Ethics and integrity

 – Openness and trust; embracing change

 – Accountability and empowerment (making it happen)

 – Teamwork.

◆ Organisations are recognising the benefits of clearly articulating core values to help guide behaviour and decision making.

◆ Influencing culture change requires obsessive attention to detail. Clear and consistent communication, and training and development are both important but the most significant factor is the role modelling of desired behaviours by managers.

Evaluate the culture of your organisation and team and assess what this means for effective management practice

◆ Handy's model defines four types of culture: power, role, network and task. A task culture is noted by Handy as the most relevant for current times, but he argued also that different areas of an organisation might benefit from different cultures.

◆ As a manager, you need to be able to read the prevailing culture of an organisation or business area and to see things from their perspective. You need to be able to adapt your behaviour to work across cultural boundaries.

◆ Managers need to recognise and manage self-interest within a subculture, so that it does not challenge the mission of the organisation as a whole.

▶▶ More @

Harvard Business Review on Culture and Change (2002), **Harvard Business School Press**
This unique collection looks at the often messy and difficult process of changing workplace culture. The articles examine why there is resistance to change on the corporate and individual level.

Semler, R. (1993), *Maverick!* **Random House**
Ricardo Semler's inspiring tale of his 'quest' to run his company in the interest of all it's stakeholders.

Buchanan, D. and Huczynski, A. (2004) *Organisational behaviour,* **FT Prentice Hall**
A comprehensive, general grounding on the mindset of people in organisations.

Schein, E. (2004) *Organisational culture and leadership,* **Pfeiffer Wiley**
Easy-to-read, practical guide packed full of ideas, tools and techniques for influencing culture.

3 Influence and relationships

Without influence, leadership does not exist, Peter Guy Northouse

We started this book by looking at the difference between leading and managing. Leadership we established is about the social skills of relationship building and influence, and management about the technical skills of maintaining systems and processes. Building leadership capacity is now mission critical for many organisations.

◆ People on the front line are more empowered. With greater empowerment has come the need for a style of leadership that guides and supports workers to make the right decisions.

◆ Project, matrix and partnership working mean that as a professional you are often likely to find yourself in a leadership role with people over whom you have no management authority. Being able to lead without the power of position is now a common leadership challenge.

◆ With employers no longer able to offer a job for life, employees have become more responsible for their long-term interests. They have views and goals that are more likely to diverge from those of the organisation and as a manager you need to be able to win their loyalty and commitment.

Increasingly leadership has become a form of influence. It is about being able to align people behind a common objective. It is about influencing people to work co-operatively, collaboratively and with mutual trust.

This is the first of two themes on leadership. In this theme, you learn how to influence people with techniques of influence and persuasion, and in the next you explore how you can release the energy of your team by empowering them to share leadership and take personal responsibility.

The definition of leadership as influence raises an interesting question. Why is it that some people seem able to influence people to behave in ways that go beyond mere compliance with the rules and routines of the organisation? Stephen Covey (1999) argues that the secret of influencing is to 'think win/win'.

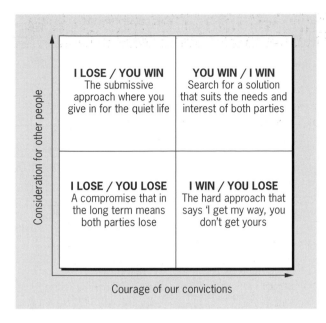

Figure 3.1 *Paradigms of influencing*

Covey suggests that whether we aim for the win/win outcome depends partly on the balance that we strike between or self-interest and our consideration for other people. So at the heart of our ability to influence lies our aptitude for developing constructive working relationships. Relationships and influence form the focus for this theme.

You will:

◆ discover how to build your personal power and broaden your range of influencing tactics

◆ learn how to adjust your communication style to improve your interactions with other people

◆ assess your Emotional Intelligence and explore its importance to building effective relationships

◆ explore how your beliefs can act as a barrier in relationships and how you can manage this.

Power and influence

Power is a crucial dimension of leadership that helps to explain why different people have different degrees of influence. The concept of power often evokes negative impressions. It can infer that people are being dominated, manipulated or coerced. However power almost always exists in organisations and as you'll see in this section, recognising and understanding how to use it is actually a very healthy thing to do.

The terms power and influence are often used interchangeably but they are different. Power is the force you use to make things happen, whereas influence is what you have when you exercise power. The most obvious example is the power that your position as a manager gives you with your team. But there are many instances in which you need to influence people over whom you have no authority:

◆ You are heading a cross functional team and have to get people outside your area co-operating, but they're not too keen.

◆ You've got a great idea but you can't get the attention of your boss who is always in meetings.

◆ You're in HR and you've got great ideas for building employee commitment but managers are too busy to attend your training programme.

So where in these scenarios does power come from? French and Raven (1968) have identified five main sources of power:

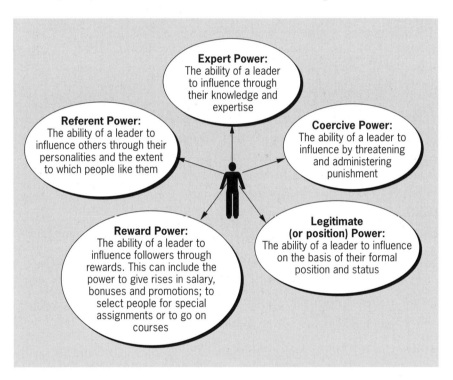

Figure 3.2 *Sources of power*

Influencing tactics

Research shows that leaders use various *influencing tactics to* convert *power* into actual *influence*. Influencing tactics are the specific behaviours that power holders use to affect others. Yukl's studies (1998) led him to identify nine key tactics. As you read through the following list, think about:

◆ which you tend to favour. Reflect on some specific incidents in your recent past to make your analysis more robust.

◆ whether you use different tactics with different people and why.

Influence tactics	Definition
Rational persuasion	Uses logical argument or factual evidence to influence others. An example would be a manager using sales figures to explain why it is more important for sales people to focus on a particular product or territory.
Inspirational appeals	Makes a request or proposal that arouses target enthusiasm by appealing to target values, ideals, and aspirations, or by increasing target self-confidence. 'We can really improve things for the staff if we do this.'
Consultation	Uses involvement as a tactic to strengthen member commitment. 'What do you think?'
Ingratiation	Uses praise, flattery, friendly behaviour, or helpful behaviour to get the target in a good mood or to think favourably of him or her when asking for something.
Personal appeals	Appeals to target feelings of loyalty and friendship toward him or her when asking for something. 'I really need you to help me on this one.'
Exchange	Offers an exchange of favours, indicates willingness to reciprocate at a later time, or promises a share of the benefits if the target helps accomplish a task. 'Thanks, I'll make sure this is reflected in your bonus.'
Coalition tactics	Seeks the aid of others to persuade the target to do something, or uses the support of others as a reason for the target to agree also. 'The consultant thinks that this is a really good idea...'
Legitimating tactics	Claims the authority or right to make the request, or verifies that it is consistent with organisational policies, rules, practices, or traditions.
Pressure	Uses demands, threats, frequent checking, or persistent reminders to influence the target to do what he or she wants.

Table 3.1 *Ten tactics for influencing (Yukl, 1998)*

Building your power base

There is a direct correlation between the influencing tactics that a manager can use and their sources of power.

As a manager you have the power that derives from your formal position. This give you the authority to ask someone to do something (legitimating tactics) or to offer an exchange (if you do this, then I'll...), or to use pressure tactics if they don't agree.

But then there is the personal power that comes from a relationship (referent power) or through your expertise (expert power). This personal power is key for effective leadership. If you have focused on growing your personal power bases, you will have a far wider range of influencing tactics available to you. Someone with referent power, for example, might choose to build on their relationship and to use ingratiation, personal appeals, exchange or positive esteem, whereas someone with expert power will be able to use rational persuasion to gain influence.

Enhancing your ability to use a wide range of influencing tactics gives you options. Some people will respond better to rationality, others when you flatter them or appeal to their dreams. Some tactics will work better in a particular organisational culture than another. By cultivating your powerbases, you'll be able to select influencing tactics to suit the situation.

Anne was recently appointed as head of a business division at a global food company. The division was in crisis. It had not made its sales or profit targets for three years. Morale was miserable; mistrust and resentment were rampant and there was open conflict between managers in the division. Anne's brief was clear; turn the division round or we'll close it.

Anne recognised that she had only a short time to demonstrate effective leadership and to build rapport and trust. She knew that she needed to understand what was not working and so her first task was to listen to key people. During her first week, she met with each manager in the division. Although she was keen to get the facts, her focus was more on getting to know each manager as a person (*referent power*). She explored their lives, dreams and aspirations and talked to them about how she could help them achieve what they wanted in their careers.

She followed the one to one meetings with an offsite meeting. The aim here was team building so that everyone would own whatever solution emerged. She encouraged everyone to express freely their complaints and reservations and then she moved the group into solution mode. Anne was able to bring some of her own experience *(expert power)* to bear in these discussions. Then with the vision in place, Anne herself moved into manager mode assigning accountability (*legitimate power*). In doing so, she took into account, as far as she could, what she knew each manager wanted to do (*reward power*).

Over the next few weeks, her stance was authoritative. She continually articulated the group's vision in a way and reminded people how his or her role was crucial to its success. Given the urgency of the situation, there were times when Anne had to use her *coercive power* with people who missed their commitments. 'A challenge of this scale was always going to demand focus and determination' she commented.

Anne has built a strong power base from which she can influence and serve the needs of her division and the organisation as a whole. By doing so, she has established herself as a strong and solid leader, able to deploy a wide range of tactics and styles to get things done. This is crucial. Power is necessary in using resources to meet goals and an essential part of a manager's job is to build a broad base of power and influence.

Network power

Another type of personal power that is becoming increasingly vital to managers is the power of the network. Network power according to Quinn (2002) is the information and influence you can access through the people who know and trust you – and through all the people those people know. This grand total of all the knowledge and influence wielded by the people you know who are willing to make their knowledge and influence available to you is your social network.

Why has this become so important and why didn't French and Raven recognise it in their analyses? The primary reason is the growing complexity of working life. In modern organisations, we all now need to be embedded in a network of contacts who know things and people that we don't.

Activity 8
Building the power of your network

Objective

This activity aims to help you plan how you can increase your influence with key people by strengthening your power in key relationships and amongst your network.

Task

1. Create your wheel of influence below by writing down the names of the key relationships that you hold in a circle around you. Include people who report to you, your peers, your managers and key collegues.

 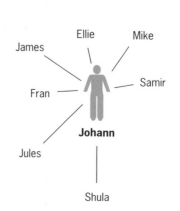

You

James   Ellie   Mike

Fran   Samir

Jules   **Johann**

Shula

2. Now analyse the strength of your network:

    –   does it contain at least two people you can trust to give you honest feedback?

    –   are there at least two people at a more senior level to yourself who will meet with you at short notice to discuss your ideas and give you advice?

    –   does it contain at least one contact person in each of the key departments/ teams you work with?

    –   who are your allies?

    –   who are your enemies?

    –   who competes with you?

3. Which working relationships do you need to improve? How can you build your referent or expert power? Develop a plan for improving your relationship below.

Feedback

The more you think about these questions, the more you will begin to see gaps within your network. You can then decide how you can get to know more people, let them know who you are and what you do. Building effective networks and working relationships will help you to build your personal power and your capacity to influence relationships. At a relationship level, your plan will need to be tailored to the level, role and nature of the person. The following lists offer some tips and techniques that you can adapt to your situation.

Managers

◆   Find out about your manager's priorities

◆   Ask for their advice

◆   Point out ways in which managers can make better use of your skills to meet priorities

◆   Look for ways to solve problems that your manager is facing

- Show appreciation for things they do to help
- Offer and ask for constructive feedback – look back to Activity 2 on the Johari window
- Be loyal

Peers

- Find ways to help peers reach their goals and look and feel successful
- Try to understand their problems and share useful information
- Look for common goals you can mutually pursue
- Form informal problem-solving groups between units
- If you are working with large groups, try to identify the opinion leader and influence them first

Direct reports

- Focus on increasing their trust in you by encouraging their ideas and by listening and empathising with their concerns
- Understand their aspirations and career hopes
- Make certain they know exactly what you expect of them in their roles
- Give recognition for good performance
- Don't take the credit for their ideas
- Do everything necessary to give them the tools and techniques to do their job
- Don't pretend to know the answer when you don't
- Keep the commitments that you make
- Clarify your own role to them
- Provide constructive feedback and encourage personal development

Emotionally intelligent leadership

Daniel Goleman (1998) describes Emotional Intelligence as:

> 'The capacity for recognising our feelings and those of others, for motivating ourselves and for managing the emotions well in ourselves and in our relationships.'

> 'We are being judged by a new yardstick: not just how smart we are or by our training and expertise, but also by how well we handle ourselves and each other.'
>
> **Daniel Goleman, Working with Emotional Intelligence, 1998**

As a journalist covering the behavioural and brain sciences for the *New York Times*, Goleman had become aware of several new areas of neurological research. These showed that the parts of the brain responsible for the emotions functioned separately, but in parallel to, those parts responsible for rational thought.

This research allowed Goleman to argue that the ability to *manage* emotions so that they work in harmony with rationality is crucial to a person's success in life. In fact, Goleman argues that Emotional Intelligence matters far more than intellectual or technical expertise when it comes to distinguishing 'star performers' from average employees. Most managers, he found, have reasonable intellectual skills whereas there is much greater variation in Emotional Intelligence meaning those with well developed Emotional Intelligence are more likely to succeed.

Emotionally intelligent leaders are able to forge relationships with groups and individuals. They are self-aware, socially skilled, disciplined and able to deal capably with other people. People with emotional intelligence think before they act, focus on their goals, understand other people's emotions and have the skill to establish common ground for discussion.

A power struggle erupted when a new Ph.D. was appointed to a government think tank. He had more expertise than the others and a better network with politicians. The team leader coached the team on working together but the problems continued. She might just have blown up and demanded that they work together. Or she might just have ignored the problem and hoped it would go away. But she didn't. She worked hard to understand the underlying issues. She focused on getting to know and build rapport and trust with every member of the team and to understand what each of them wanted to achieve. Then she dealt directly and openly with the team about the interpersonal issues. She negotiated agreements on how the team would operate. All the time, she remained focused on the tasks and goals the team needed to achieve.

Goleman's model of Emotional Intelligence

Goleman's model of Emotional Intelligence consists of four fundamental capabilities: self-awareness, self-management, social awareness and relationship management.

◆ Self-awareness and self management relate to how we manage ourselves.

◆ Social awareness and relationship management determine how we handle relationships.

Each capability, in turn, is composed of specific sets of competencies. As you look through the competencies try applying them to your situation.

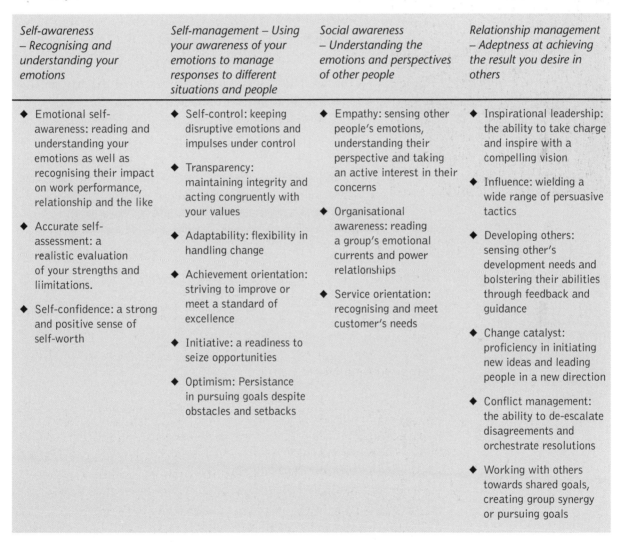

Self-awareness – Recognising and understanding your emotions	Self-management – Using your awareness of your emotions to manage responses to different situations and people	Social awareness – Understanding the emotions and perspectives of other people	Relationship management – Adeptness at achieving the result you desire in others
◆ Emotional self-awareness: reading and understanding your emotions as well as recognising their impact on work performance, relationship and the like ◆ Accurate self-assessment: a realistic evaluation of your strengths and liimitations. ◆ Self-confidence: a strong and positive sense of self-worth	◆ Self-control: keeping disruptive emotions and impulses under control ◆ Transparency: maintaining integrity and acting congruently with your values ◆ Adaptability: flexibility in handling change ◆ Achievement orientation: striving to improve or meet a standard of excellence ◆ Initiative: a readiness to seize opportunities ◆ Optimism: Persistance in pursuing goals despite obstacles and setbacks	◆ Empathy: sensing other people's emotions, understanding their perspective and taking an active interest in their concerns ◆ Organisational awareness: reading a group's emotional currents and power relationships ◆ Service orientation: recognising and meet customer's needs	◆ Inspirational leadership: the ability to take charge and inspire with a compelling vision ◆ Influence: wielding a wide range of persuasive tactics ◆ Developing others: sensing other's development needs and bolstering their abilities through feedback and guidance ◆ Change catalyst: proficiency in initiating new ideas and leading people in a new direction ◆ Conflict management: the ability to de-escalate disagreements and orchestrate resolutions ◆ Working with others towards shared goals, creating group synergy or pursuing goals

Table 3.2 *A framework for emotional competence (ei.haygroup.com)*

To be adept at achieving the results you desire in others (termed relationship management in the model), Goleman advocates that you must master the other three competencies first. The ability to influence (a relationship management competency), for example, requires the empathetic ability to gauge another person's mood and to understand their perspective (a social awareness competency).

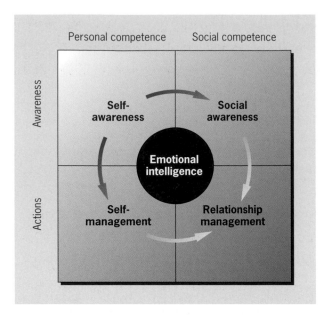

Figure 3.3 *The emotional intelligence framework*   *Source: www.ei.haygroup.com*

Activity 9
Your emotional competence

Objective

The purpose of the following activity is to provide you with an introduction to your Emotional Intelligence (EI). It is only an introduction and if you are interested to explore this area further, there are fully validated psychometric tests that will be give you a more complete picture – see the feedback for more information.

Task

Rate each question below on a scale of 1-5, according to how true it is of you. Write the appropriate number in the space before each question. Use numbers that correspond to the scale below:

1 – Never   2 – Rarely   3 – Sometimes   4 – Usually   5 – Always

1. I quickly develop an accurate idea of how another person perceives me during a particular interaction. ☐

2. I have a good network of people I can turn to, and I ask for their help when I need it. ☐

3. I am able to open up with people, not too much but enough so that I don't come across as cold and distant. ☐

4. I take time every day to reflect on what has happened. ☐

5. I inspire enthusiasm in others. ☐

6. At any given moment, I can identify the emotion I am feeling. ☐

7. I show empathy and match my feelings with those of another person in an interaction. ☐

8. I keep promises and honour commitments. ☐

9. I am generally comfortable in new situations. ☐

10. I challenge rules and procedures. ☐

11. I am clear about my own goals and values. ☐

12. I don't bury my anger or let it explode on others. ☐

13. I let go of problems, anger, or hurts from the past and don't bear grudges. ☐

14. I seek information from customers about their needs. ☐

15. I look for opportunities to help others develop new skills. ☐

16. I can effectively persuade others to adopt my point of view without pressurising them. ☐

17. I express my views honestly and thoughtfully, without being pushy. ☐

18. I take initiative and move ahead on tasks that need to be done. ☐

19. I can keep going on a big project, despite obstacles. ☐

20. I am politically astute. ☐

21. I admit my mistakes and apologise. ☐

22. I look for opportunities to improve the quality of our service. ☐

23. I can deal calmly and sensitively with the emotional displays of others. ☐

24. I try to find the positive in any given situation. ☐

Scoring the questionnaire:

Enter your ratings for each numbered question in the category where it appears.

Add the ratings for each aspect of emotional intelligence.

Self-awareness		Self-management		Total social awareness		Total relationship management	
4	____	3	____	1	____	5	____
6	____	12	____	2	____	8	____
9	____	13	____	7	____	10	____
11	___	18	____	14	____	15	____
17	___	19	____	20	____	16	____
21	___	24	____	22	____	23	____
Total	_____	**Total**	_____	**Total**	_____	**Total**	_____

Now choose a priority area for development. Looking back at the competencies and the questions to help you apply the competencies to your own situation and to think through where you think that you can improve. Make some notes on how you might achieve this.

Feedback

People can learn Emotional Intelligence.

> Life offers chance after chance to hone our emotional competence. In the normal course of a lifetime, emotional intelligence tends to increase as we learn to be more aware of our moods, to handle distressing emotions better, to listen and to empathise – in short as we become more mature.

Goleman, 1998

People who know their limitations can plan to avoid stressful situations or work around events that tug at their weaknesses. Look back at the competences in Goleman's model and think about how you use them in your role. Try to develop your thinking using the reflective learning techniques that we looked at earlier.

Emotional intelligence is a complex subject. If you found this a difficult activity you might want to ask a colleague or friend for their views on your Emotional Intelligence. Coaching is the best way to improve your Emotional Intelligence. Such development focuses on building on your strengths and correcting less desirable behaviour such as being a poor listener or being unable to control your temper. Because this process requires you to change brain-based emotional responses it can be time-consuming. A key piece of advice from Goleman is that to change your emotional responses you need to practice. If you want a new habit to stick, you have to repeat it over several months.

If you're interested to research further, try ei.haygroup.com which provides more on the Emotional Intelligence services of the HayGroup (Goleman works closely with the HayGroup to commercialise the Emotional Intelligence model).

Behavioural styles

There is a fundamental difference in how people act and respond to the world around them, how they perceive information and how they react to other people. Understanding and respecting this and being able to adapt your communications style will help you to build effective working relationships.

Earlier you might have noticed as you looked through Yukl's influencing strategies (Table 3.1) that you use different tactics with different people. This is because instinctively you are choosing to adapt your style to their personality.

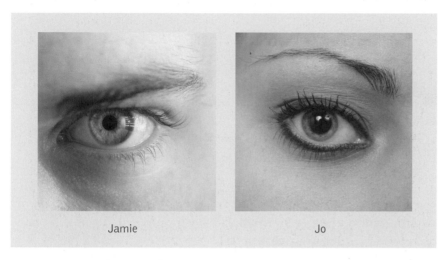

Jamie   Jo

Figure 3.4 *Conflicting perspectives*

Jamie and Jo are consultants in the same team but are very different people. Jamie is driven by instinct and the need to get results fast. This is how Jamie sees himself:

◆ willing to take risks

◆ has a good feel for things and makes decisions quickly

◆ focuses on getting things done

◆ straight with people and respected by clients.

Jo is more detailed conscious. She believes in analysing the facts before making a decision and creating plans before taking action. This is how Jo sees Jamie:

◆ not logical or analytical enough

◆ dives into things without thinking them through

◆ a bit of a liability with clients.

The way in which Jamie and Jo see and approach the world is fundamentally different. Jo might think that Jamie needs to consider the facts, but presenting him with a mass of detail to prove a point might not be the most effective approach.

A behavioural styles framework

The behavioural styles framework gives us a tool to understand people's differing points of view. DISC (www.discprofile.com) is a behavioural style analysis based on the work of Dr. William Marston who wrote The Emotions of Normal People in 1928. (He also invented the lie detector.)

> You can value the difference in other people. When someone disagrees with you, you can say 'Good! You see it differently.' You don't have to agree with them; you can simply affirm them. And you can seek to understand.'
> **Stephen R. Covey**

DISC measures people against four behavioural indicators:

> **D (for Dominance)** – how you handle problems
>
> **I (for Influence)** – how you deal with people
>
> **S (for Steadiness)** – how you pace yourself
>
> **C (for Compliance)** – how you follow rules and procedures

The real value in understanding the framework is to use it to enhance your relationships. When you are able to recognise another's style and adapt to it, you will improve communication between you and also your capacity to influence. You are basically 'talking their language'.

Most people will display elements of each style in different situations and at different times. However people will generally have a preference and a dominant style.

D personality type
Focus: RESULTS

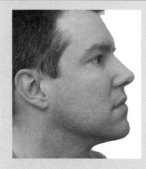

D personality types believe that achieving goals and results is the most important thing. They tend to be active, extroverted, giving the appearance of self-confidence. They like to take the initiative with others, to set the agenda and make the rules. At their best they are seen as leaders and pioneers and at their worst as aggressive, bullies and a loud mouth.

Characteristics	*You can adapt your style by:*
◆ Wants to be in charge (dislikes being told what to do)	◆ Being clear, straight, and to the point. Don't expect D type people to pick up on your feelings or unspoken agenda
◆ Sets high standards for performance	
◆ Enjoys challenges and competition	◆ Being prepared. Present your requirements, objectives, and support material without wasting their time
◆ Willing to take risks, challenge the status quo, and break the rules	◆ Being decisive and self-confidence
◆ Makes decisions quickly	◆ Avoiding telling them what to do; present them with options and ask for their opinions
◆ Doesn't mind telling people they're wrong. Can be blunt	◆ Being willing to let them have the final say

I personality type
Focus: COMMUNICATION and PEOPLE

The I personality type influence people through talking and activity. They tend to be extroverted, charming and friendly. At their best they are seen as visionaries, motivators and as a catalyst and at their worst, as a gossip or a lightweight.

Characteristics	You can adapt your style by:
◆ Optimistic, charming, and outgoing	◆ Letting them do most of the talking
◆ Energised by working with people and energises any group they are part of	◆ Looking at the big picture and avoid getting bogged down in detail
◆ Trusts people and enjoy bringing out their best	◆ Making your presentation exciting and stimulating
◆ Excellent communicator. Enjoys telling stories and tends to exaggerate	◆ Being open to new ideas and allow time to explore mutually exciting opportunities
◆ Tends to ignore the rules (since you don't think they really apply to you)	
◆ Sees the 'big picture' and can be inspirational	
◆ Dislikes details and can be scattered	

S personality type
Focus: RELATIONSHIPS and PROCESS

The S personality type tends to form strong, close and lasting relationships. They are good listeners who take time with people to make them feel at ease. They want a steady pace, security and don't like sudden change. At best they are seen as a peacemaker and a calming influence and at worst as a victim and martyr.

Characteristics	You can adapt your style by:
◆ Loyal	◆ Spending time on the relationship before jumping into the task
◆ Good listener and a team player	◆ Gently avoiding areas of disagreement and avoiding open conflict
◆ Respects the way things have always been done, and is slow to change	◆ Showing that you are listening to build their confidence
◆ Dislikes conflict and sudden change	◆ Being patient rather than pushy
◆ Patient. Stick with a project from beginning to completion	
◆ Doesn't stand up for own ideas	

C personality type
Focus: QUALITY and ACCURACY

 The C personality type adheres to rules, regulations and procedures. They believe in being accurate, detailed, rational and well-organised. At best they are seen as clear thinking, an analyst and a diplomat and at worst as nit picking, indecisive and a procrastinator.

Characteristics	*You can adapt your style by:*
◆ Researches every aspect of a situation and consider every eventuality before making a decision	◆ Getting straight down to business. Presenting the details thoroughly and avoiding hype
◆ Values being considered accurate and logical	◆ Asking their opinions, waiting for them to answer and listening to the detail
◆ Likes systems and procedures that produce predictable and consistent outcomes	◆ Being patient and giving them time to become comfortable with the situation
◆ Looks for what could go wrong	◆ Asking their help in finding facts and in developing your analysis
◆ Prefers to work alone	
◆ Has very high standards, especially for own performance. Can be a perfectionist	◆ Avoiding dropping changes on them and minimising their risk
◆ Can become paralysed and avoid taking action because of need for data	

The DISC framework helps us to understand more about ourselves and other people and to develop better relationships. Understanding the tendencies and preferences of the four styles helps you to:

◆ build on your strengths and work on your weaknesses

◆ recognise and respect that people are like to take different approaches and actions depending on their beliefs and behavioural style

◆ understand the strengths and weaknesses of others so that you can build relationships and communicate more effectively.

Activity 10
Framing your message

Objective

In this activity you assess how you can improve relationships by using the DISC behavioural styles framework.

Task

1. What is your dominant style? What are the strengths and limitations of this style?

2. Imagine that you needed to gain commitment from Jamie and Jo to a major change programme. How might you approach each of them?

Feedback

Your ability to build working relationships and to communicate effectively will be increased if you can adapt your communication style to 'speak the language' of other people. You'll probably have found that you use different styles in different situations but most people have a dominant style. Although each has positive characteristics, each can also lead to problems in relationships and communication. These are outlined in the text before this activity. Being aware of how you can adapt your style to communicate more effectively with others will help you to build trust and understanding in your relationships.

Jamie is closest to the D personality type. His focus is on getting results. Jo is closest to the C personality type. Her focus is on accuracy and quality. Compare your strategies with those that we gave earlier.

Beliefs and behaviours

In the final section of this theme we explore another important aspect of your personality that can impact on your ability to form effective working relationships – your beliefs. People tend to follow patterns of behaviour that are based on their beliefs, so beliefs are exceptionally important.

Here are just a few of the typical beliefs that influence our approach:

◆ In order for me to win, someone has to lose

◆ People love responsibility and rise to the challenge

◆ If you want something done right, do it yourself

◆ Asking for help is a sign of weakness

The interesting thing about beliefs is that often we are unaware of them or their impact. They operate at an unconscious and unquestioned level in our brain which means that they can work for or against us. For example:

Belief:	In order for me to win, someone has to lose
Behaviour:	You take a competitive and sometimes aggressive approach with others
Result:	You may get short term compliance but are unlikely to get genuine commitment
Belief:	People love responsibility and rise to the challenge
Behaviour:	You explore people's aspirations, delegate work that appeals to these and offer support
Result:	You develop an atmosphere of trust and commitment

The examples are simplistic but they illustrate a crucial point: beliefs influence behaviour, which in turn influence results

Figure 3.5 *Beliefs, behaviours and results*

Where do beliefs come from?

Many of your beliefs are formed by your early teenage years. What your parents and teachers told you, the good and bad experiences you had as a child, all these 'lay down' your core belief system. People for example often choose the same bank or political party as their parents. Think for a moment about your parents, the beliefs that you share in common with them and how these affect what you do.

Your beliefs are also shaped by your environment, the world you live in on a daily basis. If the people around you behave aggressively, some of that will rub off on you.

Finally you develop and refine your beliefs through experience and learning.

This last point is particularly important. Psychologists suggest that your ability to learn objectively from your experiences is in fact limited. They have shown that people constantly look for evidence in their experience to back their beliefs and to shrug off opposing evidence. We read newspapers that share our opinions for example. In other words we filter reality and 'see only what we want to see'.

Beliefs and assumptions

Senge uses the term 'the ladder of inference' to describe the filtering system and its impact on our behaviour. At the bottom of the ladder is the observable data that everyone can see, but as soon as we select from this data we step onto the ladder. We apply our unique set of life experiences to that data as we move up the ladder. This means that potentially we can see the same situation in a completely different way to the next person.

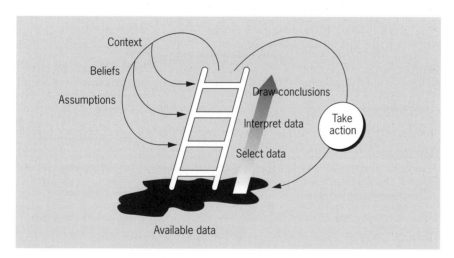

Figure 3.6 *The ladder of inference*

Returning to Jamie and Jo; Jo has been called to a meeting with her line manager Phil. Phil tells her that she needs to join the team for the next phase of Jamie's project. The initial phase of the project has been a huge success and the client is delighted with the quick wins. However it's clear that the project is far more complex than Jamie originally foresaw and the project is now running into resourcing issues. Jo's planning skills are required to bring order. By the time Jo leaves Phil's office she has climbed the ladder of inference.

Jo starts with the observable data: Phil's briefing on Jamie's project.

She selects some details from this: The project is more complex than originally anticipated.

She adds some meanings of her own (based on her beliefs about Jamie): Jamie has dived into this project headlong without thinking it through.

She moves rapidly up to assumptions: The project is in a mess before concluding, I'm being asked to pick up the pieces.

Climbing the ladder of inference seems so reasonable, and happens so quickly, that Jo is not even aware she's done it. In fact Jo is now feeling victimised. It's not the first time she's had to get involved in one of Jamie's project. Jamie gets the pick of new projects and the end result is often the same. She or someone else has to smooth over the cracks. She storms back into the office determined to show Jamie up once and for all.

Jo has only absorbed a part of the picture. Her beliefs about Jamie have prejudiced the way is which she see the situation. If Jo stops and reflects, she will realise that Phil views the project as a success worthy of further investment rather than something that needs sorting out.

Senge argues that as managers we must learn to stop short circuiting reality and see reality for what it is.

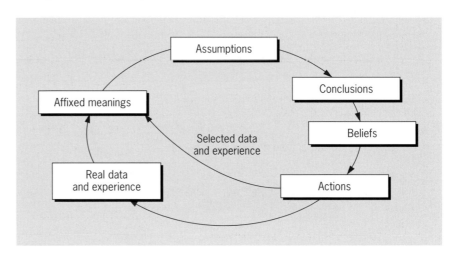

Figure 3.7 *Short circuiting reality*

You can improve your ability to do this by using the ladder of inference in three ways:

♦ Becoming more aware of your own beliefs system and how it is affecting your thinking and reasoning

♦ Making your thinking and reasoning more visible and comprehensible to others

♦ Enquiring into others' thinking and reasoning to gain a more complete picture

These three points will help you to bring openness and assertiveness into your working relationships and to work more successfully towards win-win outcomes.

Activity 11
Surfacing your beliefs

Objective

Use this activity to develop your understanding of the link between beliefs and behaviour and to explore how these impact on the behaviour and motivation of your team members.

Task

Think about a relationship that you hold that is not as effective as it might be. What beliefs do you hold about the other person and how does this impact on your behaviour with them? Try using the ladder of inference to analyse your beliefs.

I take ACTIONS based on my beliefs	
I adopt BELIEFS about the world	
I draw CONCLUSIONS	
I make ASSUMPTIONS based on the meaning I added	
I add MEANINGS (culture and personal)	
I select DATA from what I observe	
All the information in the world	

Feedback

The best way to become more consciously aware of your beliefs is to reflect on experiences and the ladder is another tool you can use alongside those we looked at in Activity 2. Once you become more consciously aware of what your beliefs are you will start to recognise when you are acting on them. For example, if you play or are interested in competitive sports you might have developed a belief that in order to win, the other party needs to lose. If you carry that belief into the workplace, albeit subconsciously, it could lead to overly competitive win-lose behaviour with colleagues.

◆ Recap

Discover how to build your personal power and broaden your range of influencing tactics

◆ Power is the force that people use to gain influence in a situation. French and Raven identified five sources of power:

- expert   - reward

- referent   - legitimate

- coercive

Other experts have added Network power.

◆ Managers who cultivate their personal powerbase (referent, expert and network power) have available a wider range of influencing tactics than those who rely on the power that comes with management position.

Assess your Emotional Intelligence and explore its importance to building effective relationships

◆ Effective leaders exhibit highly developed emotional intelligence. Emotionally intelligent leaders are skilled at building and managing relationships.

◆ Goleman has identified four key aspects of Emotional Intelligence: self-awareness, self-management, social awareness and relationship management. Goleman argues that by developing the competencies associated with each of these areas, people can enhance their Emotional Intelligence.

Learn how to adjust your style to improve your interactions with different people

◆ Effective influencers understand and accept diversity in beliefs and behavioural styles, and are able to adapt their own style 'to talk the same language' as the person they are communicating with.

◆ The DISC behavioural style framework provides an insight into different behavioural styles and can be used to help develop a range of communicating and influencing strategies.

Explore how your beliefs can act as a barrier to influencing and how you can manage this

◆ The way in which people view the world and the assumptions that they make about people and situations are determined by deep-rooted beliefs. We need to be aware of our beliefs and how they might influence our thinking.

◆ The ladder of inference is a useful way to help you think more about your inner beliefs.

▶▶ More @

Goleman, D. (2006) *Social Intelligence: The New Science of Human Relationships*, Hutchinson

Goleman, D. (1998) *Working with Emotional Intelligence, Bloomsbury*

For more on Goleman's work on Emotional Intelligence, try either of these books.

Fox, K. (2005) *Watching the English*, Hodder and Stoughton Paperbacks
Kate Fox has studied the English for 10 years and in this book she is able to identify behaviours of which most of us are only dimly aware.

O'Connor, J. and Seymour, J. (2003) *Introducing NLP Neuro-Linguistic Programming*, Harper Collins

Neuro-linguistic programming (NLP) is a psychological communication tool that is growing in popularity because of its impact on communication and influencing skills. Developing your belief systems, rapport and empathy are all challenges that NLP can help you to address.

www.discprofile.com provides more on the DISC profile including access to an online psychometric.

www.eiconsortium.org is the Consortium for Research on Emotional Intelligence in Organisations. It provides more on the work of Goleman but also other influential researchers in the Emotional Intelligence field such as Reuven Bar-On.

www.mindtools.com is an excellent website with practical resources, advice and tips on skills like questioning and listening that support your ability to influence relationships.

4 Developing a high performance culture

A front-end service employee in the Elmira, New York store recognised that Wegmans was not serving the Jewish community well and felt empowered to act on this need. He took it upon himself to go out into the community and speak with the rabbi at a local synagogue to learn what Wegmans could do to better serve this demographic. He took these ideas back to his store manager, who joined forces with the employee and accompanied him into New York City to learn even more about the Jewish community. They both came back prepared and with a plan they proposed to the division manager on new products they would like to add to the store's merchandise. Impressed with their initiative, the division manager made it happen and the store now enjoys and additional $6,000-$7,000 in revenues per week from kosher products.

Source: Great Place to Work Institute

Think of your role as a leader in comparison to that of a gardener. What does it take to grow a world-class garden? There are many variables, including events in the environment over which you have no control. But the most important principle defining your role is this: the life of the plant is within the seed, not within the gardener!
Stephen R. Covey

In situations like this, people on the front line are often closer to the information needed to make the best decisions, and organisations have a lot to gain by empowering them to do so. Numerous books and articles attest to the benefits of empowerment for both organisational effectiveness and employee well being. For many organisations, empowering staff to respond flexibly and rapidly to the needs of their customers is a potential source of competitive advantage. For the individual the reward lies in greater work satisfaction and personal development.

Often this is a lack of understanding of the empowerment concept. The 'manager role' is based on planning, organising and controlling so empowerment can feel like an abdication of this responsibility. In reality what you are doing is moving away from position power to a sharing of power and responsibility for management with your team.

Empowerment forms the focus for our final theme.

You will:

◆ explore how you can create the essential conditions for empowerment

◆ learn how to create and communicate a vision that gains the buy in of stakeholders and gives individuals a clear sense of purpose

◆ evaluate how your leadership style supports empowerment within your team

◆ apply a coaching model to develop confidence and capabilities of team members.

The conditions for empowerment

Clutterbuck (1995) cautions that all too often, empowerment is used as a pretext by organisations to mean 'shouldering more responsibility for less reward'. He suggests that empowerment should enable people to:

◆ take more control over their jobs and working environment

◆ enhance the contribution they make as individuals and members of a team

◆ seize opportunities for personal growth and self-fulfilment.

For many organisations this involves a major change of culture, systems and infrastructure and a great deal of time and investment. To merit the effort, you need at the outset to be very clear about the benefits you are seeking. Bowen and Lawler (1992) describe three bottom line gains possible from empowering service employees:

◆ Quicker responses to customer needs during service delivery.

◆ Quicker responses to dissatisfied customers during service recovery.

◆ Empowered employees can be a great source of service ideas, word of mouth advertising and customer retention.

The empowered mindset

Research (Thomas and Velthouse, 1990) shows that for empowerment to take place, people need to feel:

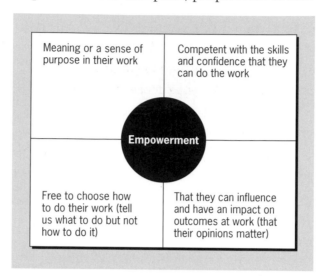

Figure 4.1 *The empowered mindset*

The key point here is that empowerment is something that takes place in the mind of the individual, it is about how the individual feels. People don't just feel empowered because the organisation tells them they are. They feel empowered because they work within an environment in which empowerment can flourish.

So, what are the conditions for empowerment? A review of the literature highlights some crucial areas:

Empowerment requires ...	But does not mean ....
A clear vision supported by an equally clear strategy and goals at all level of the organisation.	A free for all environment where people can do exactly what they want.
Effective leadership where managers nurture, coach, mentor, encourage and support people in achieving their best.	Expecting people to get it right every time.
Teamwork and trust where creativity and managed risks are encouraged, where people are encouraged to learn from mistakes and to problem solve together.	People can blame each others and make excuses when things go wrong. The freedom to take action and make decisions comes with a responsibility for people to be accountable.
Communication and information sharing where employees have the necessary information for making good decisions and taking action.	Expecting everything to be provided on tap. When people act accountably, they take ownership and responsibility for finding solutions to problems.
A high level of participation from team members on decisions and goals.	A one person: one vote democracy on every decision. Not every employee can participate in every decision.
Trust and trustworthiness where people have freedom to decide how to do their work.	A complete abdication of management. The manager must still offer support, monitor the results and provide overall co-ordination.

Table 4.1 *The nature of empowerment*

In other words it is a question of achieving a balance, a balance that works for both leader and follower.

The rest of this theme explores how you can achieve this balance. It looks specifically at:

◆ how you can create and communicate a vision that gives people a sense of purpose

◆ how you can develop motivation and build commitment through participative decision making and delegation

◆ how you can use coaching to develop the competence and confidence of team members.

By doing these things you will start to foster trust and teamwork and the conditions for empowerment.

Activity 12
Your approach to empowerment

Objective

Use this activity to start thinking about empowerment in your work environment.

Task

1. If people you work with were asked to give feedback on how effectively you empower people, what would they say? Why is this?

2. How do your beliefs affect your approach to empowerment? Read through each of the following pairs of statements and decide whether you think they apply to your team members. For each pair tick the relevant box – once – to show which one you most agree with and how much.

1 = strongly agree   2 = agree mostly   3 = agree more than disagree

	1 2 3	3 2 1	
Generally they dislike having to work	☐ ☐ ☐	☐ ☐ ☐	Generally they want to work
They need to be closely supervised	☐ ☐ ☐	☐ ☐ ☐	They can work without supervision
Generally they prefer to avoid responsibility	☐ ☐ ☐	☐ ☐ ☐	Generally they like to take responsibility
They don't have much potential to develop	☐ ☐ ☐	☐ ☐ ☐	They all have potential to develop
They only come to work to get money	☐ ☐ ☐	☐ ☐ ☐	Working fulfils a number of needs

Feedback

A manager's beliefs about what motivates your team members his or her team members has been shown to have a great impact on the extent to which he or she will encourage empowerment. McGregor (1987) believes there are two extremes of management styles. He called them 'Theory X' and 'Theory 'Y'.

If your responses are mainly in the three left-hand boxes it suggests that you lean towards Theory X. If your responses are mainly in the three right-hand boxes it suggests you lean towards Theory Y.

McGregor argues that Theory X managers believe that people dislike working and only work for money and security. For this reason, there is a lack of trust in their management approach. Management tactics might include close supervision, tight controls and telling people what to do, essentially an environment of command and control, or might be softer and rely on exchange (if you do this, then I will …). in the hope that employee will co-operate when asked to do so.

Theory Y on the others hand sets out a participative style of management that encourages empowerment. It is based on the beliefs that employees are happy to work, are self-motivated and creative, and enjoy working with greater responsibility.

> **The way you see them is the way you treat them and the way you treat them is the way they often become.**
> **Zig Ziglar**

McGregor argues that the basic assumptions of Theory X are not correct; people seek more from their work than money. He proposes that if managers seek to create Theory Y environment, where decision making and responsibility can be devolved, they will foster long term commitment rather than short term compliance. This is consistent with the thinking that we have looked at so far in relation to empowerment.

In practice it's not black and white. Few would dispute the benefits of empowerment but the reality is that not all environments are ready for it. As you think about your team, you might feel that different members need different approaches. Some may thrive on Theory Y management, while others may need Theory X management. Much will also be determined by the culture of your organisation. It can be challenging to take a Theory Y approach if you work in an organisation that values command and control as oppose to empowerment. In some environments, some forms of manufacturing for example, there is less scope for employees to become involved in decision making. The question of 'how much empowerment?' is a key one that we consider later in this section.

Crafting vision and meaning

'Vision and direction are essential for greatness. In world-class organisations, every-one has a clear sense of where the enterprise is going. Only when the leaders of an organisation know that their people understand the agreed-upon vision and direction can they attend to strengthening the organisation's ability to deliver on this vision. '

Source: *The Vision Thing: Without It You'll Never Be a World-Class Organisation*, by Ken Blanchard and Jesse Stoner

A powerful vision is an essential starting point for empowerment because it helps people to make choices with an end result in mind.

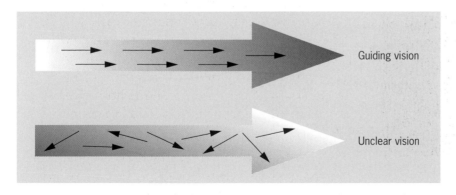

Figure 4.2 *Vision and alignment*

Vision is not the same as goals and objectives. It is a more idealised picture of what the organisation, or your area of responsibility, might become.

> If you have no vision, but only formal plans, then every unpredicted change in the environment makes you feel your sky is falling in
> **Henry Mintzberg, 1994**

Martin Luther King Jr. described his vision of a world where people live together in mutual respect. In his 'I Have a Dream' speech, he described a world where his children 'will not be judged by the colour of their skin, but by the content of their character.' He created powerful and specific images from the values of brotherhood, respect, and freedom for all.

His speech evoked vivid images and strong feelings. This is important because it is the pictures and feeling rather than the goal itself that infect people with energy and commitment.

There are plenty of examples of 'lip service' vision or statements developed as promotional tools. They might be hung publicly in entrance lobbies and used with investors and customers, but in reality they do not summon any emotion or sense of commitment amongst those who work in the organisation and do little to guide their actions.

For a vision to be effective, it needs to be:

◆ inspirational, clear and challenging

◆ focused, providing a sense of purpose

◆ future oriented

◆ guiding, providing direction without removing freedom

◆ enduring, providing a long term aim.

Source: Doherty and Hone, 2002

It should stretch expectations and aspirations and encourage people to move out of their comfort zone.

I once attended a training seminar where one of the exercises was to come up with as many ideas as we could for earning ten dollars by the end of the day. This was supposedly an exercise in brainstorming. After a few minutes, the instructor polled the audience for some of their ideas. Some ideas were better than others, but everyone agreed that even the bad ones could have earned someone ten dollars in a day.

The instructor then asked if any of the ideas presented so far could earn someone a million dollars. The consensus was that the vast majority of ideas had absolutely no chance to make anyone a million dollars, and a select few had only a very slim chance. At the end of the exercise, the instructor simply said, 'You don't get million dollar ideas from a ten dollar vision.'

In other words, the quality of your vision determines the creativity, quality and originality of your ideas and solutions.

Vision and stakeholders

Quinn (2002) suggests that a vision statement should cover three key areas:

◆ First is the case for change.

◆ Second is an ideal goal or goals – these are not so specific as to define the final outcomes but should paint a picture of the future.

◆ Third is a focus on people, both internal and external stakeholders, how the vision supports them and the role that they play.

Stakeholders are people who have an interest in or an involvement with the fulfillment of your vision. They might be internal or external to your organisation. In a school for example, stakeholders might include managers, teachers, central office and support personnel, parents, governors, pupils and community members.

Often vision is painted as the inspiration of a single heroic leader, the pathfinder, but it is rarely this way in practice. Generally speaking the more stakeholders buy into the vision, the more likely you are to achieve the outcomes you want, and so it's important to involve at least your more important stakeholders in the vision forming process. It comes down to ownership. Those stakeholders who feel that they have a stake in the vision will work harder to ensure that the outcomes are achieved.

Vision and creativity

Part of your skill as a manager is in being able to facilitate the vision forming process. Most vision forming activities start with some form of gathering, and if this is to become a creative exploration of ideas, it needs careful consideration.

Facilitation tips and techniques for vision forming

♦ Post-it notes are a great way to kickstart a discussion. Ask future focused questions like, 'Where is this industry headed and how do we need to be succeed in the future?' and then ask participants to work in pairs or trios and note their initial ideas. These can then be collected, grouped and used as the basis for discussion or even for creating the agenda.

♦ Ask people to draw the future or to create stories about it.

♦ Every once in a while it is good to break up the group dynamics (especially if the group is quiet) by asking people to work in a different way. Suggest that participants form pairs or trios for a few minutes. Use this as an opportunity to discuss a particular issue, asking participants to report back on their musings once they return to the larger group.

♦ A useful way of stimulating new thoughts is to allocate different 'roles' within the discussion from time to time. This can encourage people to 'see' the issue from different perspectives. Try for example, asking people to take opposing viewpoints in a discussion or suggest that someone play Devil's advocate for a few minutes, or lateral thinker or positive thinker.

♦ Pay close attention to the tone of the meeting and to how the participants are feeling. Good vision statements emerge from upbeat meetings. Time out is a very useful technique when hidden agendas, unspoken antagonisms, body language or other examples of bad atmosphere are getting in the way of the discussion. Take a 1-2 minute pause. In that time ask each person to reflect on the following questions:

a) How am I feeling at this moment?

b) Is there anything that I wish I had said or done, but didn't? If so, why?

c) What would I like more of...and less of from the others in the room?

Then ask people how they responded to questions b & c. Resume the discussion once everyone has been heard.

♦ If you are aware of lots of intense feelings within the group (e.g. the topic is one about which people are likely to feel strongly) you could begin by giving each participant the chance to express their views upfront so they don't get in the way of the subsequent conversation. The deeper the feelings the more likely they are to 'leak out' in unhelpful ways during the proceedings. (Sly comments, diversionary discussions etc...). An alternative is to collect such issues as they are raised and note them on a flip chart or issues board. In this way you can value the contribution without it undermining the flow of the meeting.

You'll need to be patient and keep working at it. It can take time to unearth, polish and refine the vision. The analogy of the lightning bolt is not a particularly realistic one!

Connecting people to the vision

With the vision in place, you need to build a sense of commitment. Earlier we saw that people need to find meaning and a sense of purpose in the vision and this is exactly what effective managers enable people to do.

This might be on a 1:1 basis or through a workshop or presentation. What is essential is that you paint a picture that is sufficiently vivid that it enables people to sense through their imagination what the future might look like. You are communicating the feelings that go with the vision with the intention of inspiring the same feelings in others.

> **Thou shalt not is soon forgotten, but 'once upon a time' will last forever.**
> **Philip Pulman**

Stories are an excellent tool for communicating with people, and are something that you can prepare in advance and practice until the words come naturally. Stories are powerful because they engage with people's feelings and help them to learn, absorb, remember and share information and ideas. They don't have to be long or funny, they just need to convey a message.

Talking about his vision for customer service, the manager recounted the time he and his wife checked into a hotel bedroom. On the pillow was the usual feedback form, but under the section that read 'Was The Room Cleaned To Your Satisfaction?' was a hand-written note saying, 'Please look under the bed – Betty'.

Much to his wife's amusement the man started scrabbling under the bed, and found, right in the middle, a small card. On it was written: 'I've cleaned under here as well – Betty'.

Activity 13
Vision, stakeholders and commitment

Objective

Use this activity to reflect on the previous section and to think about your vision for your team and how you can help people to connect with it.

Task

1. What is your vision for the future of your area? How does it fit with your organisation's vision as a whole? How does it serve your stakeholders?

2. How well connected are people around you to the vision? How could you help them to be more connected?

Feedback

1. Having a vision for your area is important but so is the issue of alignment. Your vision needs to be aligned with that of your organisation and the objectives of your key stakeholder groups. Stakeholder groups you could consider include:

    ◆ employees

    ◆ managers

    ◆ suppliers

    ◆ customers

    ◆ service users

    ◆ regulators

    ◆ owners and investors

    ◆ local community.

    One of the problems with stakeholder analysis is that the requirements and expectations of different groups can conflict. It can become impossible to come up with something that meets what everyone wants and which has a realistic focus. The interest-influence grid can be used to distinguish the most critical stakeholders.

	Low Influence	High Influence
High Interest	Useful group for bouncing ideas off.	Key group – how can you build on their interest and influence by involving them?
Low Interest	Lowest priority group – might be important to keep them informed, particularly if your decision has an adverse impact on them.	Important group – how can you raise their interest and involve them?

Figure 4.4 *Stakeholder mapping*

2. Connecting with the vision is crucial. Think for a moment about what your organisation's vision means to you personally and how it fits with your own goals. How does it drive your behaviour? If you have this sense of connection, then how are you translating this to your team? If you don't then can you expect your team to have it? If people are to be empowered effectively, then they need to understand the overall direction and feel a sense of purpose in it. Evidence suggests that your actions and behaviours as a role model are more crucial in helping them to understand this than any other factor.

How participative is your leadership style?

Empowerment means that people are more involved in the design of their work and in the decisions that affect them. As a result they feel more ownership. As you consider how to involve people in decision making, you face three broad questions:

When should I involve others in decision making?

Four possible areas that you could consider include:

- goal setting. Team members can help establish goals for themselves, for a specific task or for the team as a whole

- selecting a course of action e.g. which equipment to buy

- solving specific problem such as customer complaints

- making policy decision that affect the team or the organisation e.g. flexible working, recruitment, communication.

Who should participate?

Firstly individuals might make decisions on their own, or they may pair up with a manager to form a decision-making team e.g. to set objectives. Employees may also participate in a decision-making group. This may be formal as in quality circles or may be informal with members of a group expressing opinions in order to reach some consensus.

Just how participative should decision making be?

Tannenbaum and Schmidt (1973, updated 1991) were among the first to consider this question. They developed a scale which reflected the degree of control that a manager exercises over decision making with the team.

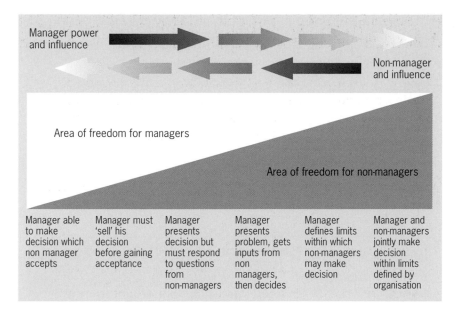

Figure 4.5 *The leadership continuum*

At the far left of the scale is an **autocratic** leadership style with no delegated freedom at all. At the far right is a more **democratic** style where individuals are able not only to make decisions but to determine, within agreed boundaries, what decisions are needed and when to take them.

Take a look at the following decisions and for each of them, use the continuum to decide what your approach would be and why?

1. You have been asked whether you will commit your group to additional work. It would call for working erratic hours and would impact on the lifestyle of group members. Successful completion of the task would improve things in the long run, but to commit and fail would have serious implications.

2. A customer has raised a very technical issue which requires the expertise of specialists beyond your team. Although the issue will affect the way in which your team works, you do not believe they have the training and experience to contribute to the decision – even though they think they know the answer.

3. One of the members in your team, although experienced is reluctant to take responsibility for decisions. His attitude is 'You are paid to manage. I am paid to do the work. You make the decisions.' You have an important customer complaint that you want him to take on and resolve and you believe he has the knowledge to do it.

4. A series of problems has arisen and need to be resolved. You have some ideas what is causing them but it is your team that is intimately familiar with the problems, the advantages and disadvantages of possible solutions etc…

Tannenbaum and Schmidt suggest that three factors determine your decision making approach in any given scenario:

◆ **Yourself** – your own natural preferences

◆ **The task**. Higher levels of involvement are called for when employee acceptance is necessary. This is the case in Scenario 1. Complex decisions require more consultation whereas simple ones are straightforward to delegate. Time pressures also have an impact. Generally speaking unilateral action is faster than participative decision making.

◆ The **readiness of your followers**. Readiness has two aspects:

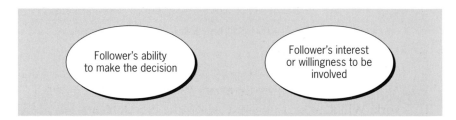

Follower's ability to make the decision

Follower's interest or willingness to be involved

Figure 4.6 *Follower readiness*

When ability is low as in Scenario 2 delegation is likely to result in a poor quality decision. You are more likely to retain control of the final decision, although you might consult with the team and use it as a coaching opportunity.

Similarly when willingness is low, as in Scenario 3, delegation is a high risk strategy. A more participative style where you jointly develop a solution might develop the individual's confidence and motivation.

When the followers are able and willing as in Scenario 4, you can move across the scale and delegate the decision.

Empowerment and delegation

There is an important difference between empowerment and delegation and it comes back to the empowered mindset that we set out at the start of this theme. For empowerment to work, people must *want* and *be able* to take more control over their jobs and to enhance the contribution they make as individuals and members of a team. They must be in a high state readiness.

This is because empowerment comes with a caveat which is that individuals are willing to become personally accountable for their choices and actions. When people are accountable they say 'What can I do to make this work?', 'It was my mistake, here's what I'll do next time' rather than 'That's not our fault, it's down to…' or 'I didn't have the information, so I had to give up.'

Delegation, on the other hand, is a technique that you can use to make people responsible for specific tasks. If you can delegate responsibility then you'll achieve two things. First you'll free up your own time to focus on managing rather than doing. Second through effective delegation you can develop the capability, motivation and confidence of your team members. People tend to thrive on responsibility and it follows that the more effectively you delegate, the more accountable the people in your team will become.

Five steps to delegation

1. *Define the task*
   To begin you need to clarify what the job involves. It's worth thinking of tangible outputs – evidence that will show when the work has been done – and timescales.

2. *Select the individual or team*
   Who has the right skills and time to do the work? It's also important to think about who might benefit most from doing the work. Will it be an opportunity for one of your team to develop new skills and broaden their experience?

3. *Briefing*
   The next – and possibly most crucial – stage is to brief the person effectively. In briefing, you are trying to do four things.

   ◆ To generate enthusiasm for the task (by creating meaning).

   ◆ To agree outcomes.

   ◆ To agree what resources such as people, materials are necessary for success.

   ◆ To agree a framework and timescale for the task.

   You need to consider just how much responsibility you will delegate and to set the limits. For example, you may set the objectives and timescale yourself, but allow the other person scope to choose methods and who else to involve.

   At this point you may need to confirm understanding (with the other person) of the previous points, and to get their ideas. As well as showing you that the job can be done, this helps to reinforce commitment.

4. *Reviewing progress and providing support*
   During the period when the task is being carried out you should offer support, if it is needed, and monitor the task or project to make sure it stays on track. Methods of checking and controlling should be agreed in advance otherwise it will seem like interference or lack of trust.

5. *Feedback on results*
   It is essential to let the person know how they are doing, and whether they have achieved their aims. If not, you need to review with them why things did not go to plan, and deal with the problems. Think about your own role in the process. How did you brief the person? Did you give them enough or too

> **People are not stupid and can recognise the difference between dumping and delegation**
> **Steve Morris, Graham Willcocks and Eddy Knasel**

much responsibility? What would you do differently next time?

These last two steps are often the most poorly executed, but they are key and will demand significant energy on your part as a manager. Without monitoring and feedback, you are not delegating just allocating tasks.

Activity 14
Your leadership style

Objective

This activity will help you to think more about your leadership style and the extent to which you are able to vary it.

Task

1. Identify tasks that you have delegated to two different people recently. For each, tick a point on the continuum below to show how you briefed the person doing the work. How participative was your approach and what might you do differently?

Task 1	You decide	They decide
Setting objectives	_____	_____
Choosing methods	_____	_____
Deciding resources and who else to involve	_____	_____
Setting the timeframe	_____	_____
Deciding when and how to review progress	_____	_____

Task 2	You decide	They decide
Setting objectives	_____	_____
Choosing methods	_____	_____
Deciding resources and who else to involve	_____	_____
Setting the timeframe	_____	_____
Deciding when and how to review progress	_____	_____

2. Effective managers need to be able to flex their style but most managers will have styles that feel more comfortable than others. At what point on the continuum would you place yourself?

Your leadership style

←——————————————————————————————————→

Autocratic
You prefer to make your own decisions and give staff specific instructions

Consultative
You seek out opinions from staff but you make the final decision yourself

Participative
You prefer to come to agreement about the best way forward with your team

Democtratic
You may allow the group to make the decision themselves

Feedback

Although you might favour a particular leadership style, it is unlikely that your style is purely autocratic, consultative, participative or democratic. There is no consistent evidence that any given position on this dimension of leadership style is the best one and it is generally agreed that the most appropriate style is the one that gets results in a situation.

That said, there is general acceptance that an autocratic style of management is unlikely to yield results in the long term. Today's manager is likely to find that team members resent being treated as subordinates and that they expect to be consulted and to have an influence. It's not unusual for employees to be highly critical of the organisational systems that demand their loyalty and as a manager you need to win their commitment. This is particularly true if you are seeking to encourage a climate of accountability in which empowerment can thrive.

Coaching, questioning and feedback

> **I want everyone to get up in the morning and have self respect that in the job they do, they're doing a good job.**
> **Charles Dunstone, Chief Executive, Carphone Warehouse**

Coaching is a powerful tool that you can use to develop the skills and confidence of team members, which in turn will promote individual responsibility and accountability. Almost eight out of ten respondents who responded to a survey from the Chartered Institute of Personnel and Development (CIPD) (2006) reported that they now use coaching and of those, the vast majority considered it be effective or very effective as a means of personal development.

What is coaching?

There is no precise definition, but there are some generally agreed characteristics of coaching in organisations.

Coaching:

- is a collaborative learning relationship
- uses the workplace and its challenges as a vehicle for learning
- focuses on the specific and identified development needs of an individual in his or her own work context
- provides people with feedback on both their strengths and their weaknesses
- has built in flexibility so that it can be used in short session that fit with the constraints of the workplace
- is a skilled activity.

Antonioni (2000) explains that coaching is commonly used for two purposes:

- **Performance management coaching** which occurs when there is a gap between an individual's current performance and the way he or she should perform.
- **Performance enhancement coaching** when an individual is meeting performance requirements but wants to perform at a higher level.

Performance management coaching tends to be led by the coach.

The coaching cycle

Most coaching activities follow a simple three step cycle:

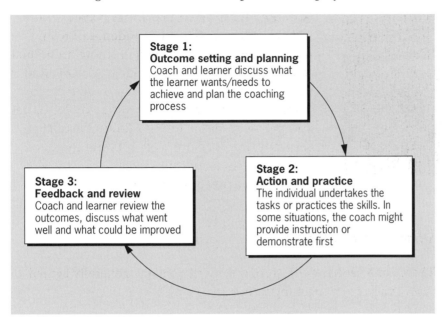

Figure 4.7 *The coaching cycle*

In situations where the coach is showing the learner how to do something, the coach might take the lead, helping the learner to set outcomes, demonstrating the task and then providing directive feedback about what the learner needs to do next.

It other situations, it can be the learner who takes the lead, and in most situations coaching will be more effective if the learner has ownership of and responsibility for the process at some level.

As coaching becomes led by the learner, the fundamental skill lies not in being the expert but in being able to challenge and use careful questioning to encourage the learner to explore their situation and what they want to achieve. The coach's role is essentially as a catalyst, helping the learner see the situation through new eyes.

Questioning and challenging

One of the most widely used models for structuring the first part of the coaching cycle shown above is called GROW (Whitmore, 1992). GROW is an acronym for Goal, current Reality, Options and Will – which are seen as the four key elements of a coaching session.

Firstly, a coaching programme must have a Goal or outcome to be achieved. The Goal should be as specific as possible and it should be possible to measure whether it has been achieved.

You need to know where you are starting from – the current Reality. It is surprising how often this becomes the key part of a coaching session and that by just seeing clearly the situation (rather than as the learner imagined the situation to be), the solution becomes obvious and straightforward.

Once you know where you are and where you want to go, the next step is to explore what Options you have for getting there and to choose the best.

Finally you need to explore the learner's Will to make the journey. The desired outcome from this stage is a commitment to action. On a scale of 1-10, if their Will is less than 8, you need to go back round the cycle. Can you break the goal down into smaller steps?

Grow	Setting clear goals for learning
Reality	Checking and raising awareness of the situation right now
Options	Finding alternative strategies, solutions, answers
Will	Testing, commitment and next steps

Figure 4.8 The GROW model

GOALS
Setting goals for the learning project in general, or for this particular coaching session

What exactly do you want to achieve (short/long term)

- How much of this is within your control?
- How well are you doing now, on a scale of 1-10?
- How will you know you've achieved it?

REALITY
Checking and raising awareness of the situation right now

Why haven't you reached this goal already?

- Are there any constraints outside yourself which stop you moving towards this goal?
- How might you overcome them?
- What's really stopping you?

OPTIONS
Finding alternative strategies, solutions, answers

What could you do to move towards this goal? What else could you do? And what else? (keep repeating this!)

◆ If time and resources were not a factor – what could you do?

◆ What would happen if you did nothing?

◆ Is there anybody whom you admire and respect who does this really well? What do they do that you could try?

WILL (and **WHAT**, **WHEN** and by **WHOM**)
Testing your commitment to your goal, making concrete, realistic plans to reach it

Which of all options will you choose? (Maybe several)

◆ Who else needs to help and support you in your plan?

◆ What obstacles do you expect to meet? How will you overcome them?

◆ When specifically will you take the first step in your plan?

Towards a coaching culture

A good coach can also be instrumental in spreading a 'coaching culture" throughout the organisation. That is, once an individual manager has honed his or her skills, that same manager can then coach others how to coach.

In a coaching culture, coaching can flow in all directions from all parties within a team, between teams as well as up and down the organisation:

◆ Line managers provide performance and development coaching for their direct reports

◆ Peers provide support for each other's learning and problem solving within a team or between teams

◆ Upwards coaching although this does rely on the manager being open and willing to receive upward feedback.

Introducing coaching competencies into an organisation is a very powerful strategy to create an adaptive workplace culture committed to the ongoing process of development and learning. But, for it to happen the culture within the organisation must value and be enthusiastic to use feedback as a learning tool. So, how do you create a coaching climate? Clutterbuck (2005) has some suggestions:

◆ **Ensure that all managers have the basic skills of coaching** and that they put them into practice. Good practice typically involves follow up group sessions, or the use of a mastercoach to sit in on coaching sessions and provide immediate feedback.

◆ **Equip all employees with the skills to be coached effectively.** The more the learner understands about the coaching process, the easier it becomes for the coach to help them.

◆ **Develop mastercoaches** to help managers grow in their coaching skills.

◆ **Recognise and reward managers who demonstrate good coaching practice.**

◆ **Measure and provide feedback on the quality, relevance and accessibility of coaching.** 'What coaching is happening?', 'How effective is it?'. Identifying pockets of good and bad practice allows for remedial action.

◆ **Ensure that top management provide strong, positive role models.** Unless people see top management investing in their own development, and in coaching others, their own motivation will inevitably be muted.

◆ **Identify cultural and systems barriers to developmental behaviours.** Top of the list of excuses that managers give for not devoting sufficient attention to coaching is time. Particularly relevant is how managers perceive the overall importance of coaching in relation to other priorities is the overall supportiveness of the organisation towards development.

Establishing a coaching climate, requires a concentrated and integrated approach. For real change to happen, managers need a progressive level of skills improvement, access to just-in-time sources of advice, pressure from coaches, positive role models and a supportive environment.

Clutterbuck's advice is aimed at organisations, but you can adapt it to grow a coaching culture within your team.

Activity 15
Developing a coaching culture

Objective

Use this activity to think through how you might develop your own coaching skills and the skills of others within your team.

Task

1. How effective are you as a role model for coaching in your team and how could you become even more effective?

2. Identify a learning need within your team and select someone from within your team who could act as a coach.

3. What skills will the individual need to act as an effective coach?

Feedback

A positive example from you is critical. You might choose to seek feedback and coaching from a member of your own team and demonstrate your openness and willingness to learn.

By developing coaching capabilities within your team you greatly increase the potential for people to learn and develop together; the learning organisation. Clutterbuck suggests that as well as focusing on the skills of those who will act as coach you need to raise awareness amongst the people to be coached.

> **Coaching is a profession of love. You can't coach people unless you love them.**
> **Eddie Robinson**

Evidence suggests that learners value a number of skills and qualities in a coach:

◆ They show a genuine interest in the learner.

◆ The give the learner confidence that they can meet the challenge.

◆ They are prepared to give time to the person.

◆ They are able to help the learner gain access to different experiences and learning opportunities.

◆ Through careful questioning, they can help the learner reflect and think about what they can realistically achieve.

◆ They are prepared to give feedback that is genuinely useful.

◆ Recap

Explore how you can create the essential conditions for empowerment

◆ Empowerment means that people are more involved in their work and in the decisions that affect them. The benefit is that they have greater ownership of what they need to achieve and become accountable for achieving the outcomes.

◆ For people to feel empowered, managers must create an environment in which empowerment must flourish. A clear vision, a participative leadership style and a coaching climate in which people can develop both their confidence and competence are core elements of this environment.

Learn how to create and communicate a vision that gains the buy in of stakeholders and gives individuals a clear sense of purpose

◆ A clear vision is important because it helps people to make the right choices. A vision that takes into account the needs and objectives of key stakeholders will have greater levels of ownership and commitment to achieving the outcomes.

◆ Managers need to role model the vision and take every opportunity to reinforce it.

Evaluate how your leadership style supports empowerment within your team

◆ For managers to be able to meet the demands of the various leadership situations in which they find themselves, they need to be able to flex their style between being autocratic, consultative, participative and democratic.

- In an empowered environment, managers share power and decision-making with their team, and a participative or democratic leadership style is likely to be most effective.

- The extent to which leaders are able to delegate tasks and decision making depends on three factors: their own beliefs and feelings about a situation, the nature of the situation itself and the readiness of followers.

Apply a coaching model to develop confidence and capabilities of team members

- Coaching is a powerful technique for developing follower readiness. It uses the workplace to help develop a learner to meet his or her individual learning needs.

- Although most frequently coaching takes place between a line manager and his or her direct reports, a number of organisations are trying to foster a climate of coaching where people throughout the organisation are open to and able to give feedback to their peers and line managers.

▶▶ More @

Whitmore, Sir J. (1992) *Coaching for performance*, Nicholas Brealey Publishing
This book provides a simple foundation for coaching based on developing awareness and responsibility through asking questions and listening. The G R O W model of coaching – Goal, Reality, Option, Will – is presented as a format for coaching sessions.

Clutterbuck, D. (2005) *Making Coaching Work: Creating a Coaching Culture*, Chartered Institute of Personnel and Development
Coaching can only work when the culture is supportive: where managers, coaches and coachees all trust each other and are working together. Clutterbuck talks you through the groundwork.

Lashley, C. (2002) *Empowerment: HR strategies for service excellence*, Butterworth Heinemann
This book uses case studies from companies such as McDonalds, TGI Fridays and Harvester Restaurants to build a picture of empowerment of service employees in context, illustrating how different forms of empowerment are employed and different working arrangements are practiced.

www.cipd.co.uk, the website of the Chartered Institute of Personnel and Development offer free fact sheets and reports on many of aspect of empowerment.

There are a number of other titles within the Management Plus series that are particularly relevant to empowerment. These include Leading Teams, Managing Information and Meeting goals through Innovation.

References

Antonioni, D. (2000) Leading, Managing and Coaching, *Industrial Management*, September

Bennis, W. (1998) *On becoming a leader*, Arrow

Bowen and Lawler (1992) The empowerment of service workers, what, why, how and when, *Human Resource Management and Industrial Relations*, Vol 33 No 3.

Clutterbuck, D. (1995) *The power of empowerment*, Kogan Page

Clutterbuck, D. (2005) *Making Coaching Work: Creating a Coaching Culture*, Chartered Institute of Personnel and Development

Covey, S. (1999) *The 7 habits of Highly Successful People*, Simon and Schuster

Covey, S. (1999) *Principle Centred Leadership*, Simon and Schuster

Doherty, T. and Hone, T. (2002), *Managing Public Services*, Routledge

Drucker, P. (2005) Managing Oneself, *Harvard Business Review*, Vol 83, No 1, pp 100-109

Drucker, P. (2000) Managing Knowledge Means Managing Oneself, *Leader to Leader*

French, J. P. R. Jr., and Raven, B. (1960) The bases of social power, D. Cartwright and A. Zander (eds.), *Group dynamics* (pp. 607-623). New York: Harper and Row

Great Place to Work Institure, (2006) *The Power of Storytelling in a Great Place to Wor*k

Goleman, D. (1998) *Working with emotional intelligence*, Bloomsbury

Handy, C. (1993) *Understanding Organisations*, Penguin Business Library

Kotter, J. (1990) *A force for change: How leadership differs from management*, The Free Press

Kouzes and Posner (2002) *The Leadership Challenge*, Jossey Bass Wiley

Leader Values (www.leader-values.com)

Lynch, R. (1997) *Corporate Strategy*, FT Prentice Hall

McGregor, D. (1987) *The Human Side of Enterprise*, Penguin

Mintzberg, H. (1973) *The Nature of Managerial Work*, Harper & Row

Nadler, D. and Tushman, M. (1997), *Competing by Design*, Oxford University Press

Pedlar, M., Burgoyne, J. and Boydell, T. (2001) *A Manager's Guide to Self Development*, MCGraw Hill

Plant, R. (1987) *Managing Change and Making it Stick*, Fontana

Poole, E. and Carr, M. (2005) *If I knew then what I know now!, The Ashridge Journal*, Spring 2005

Quinn, R., Faerman, S., Thompson, M. and McGrath, M. (2002), *Becoming a Master Manager*, Wiley

Senge, P. (1990) *The Fifth Discipline: The Art & Practice of The Learning Organisation*, New York: Currency Doubleday

Schein, E. (1988) *Organisational Psychology*, 3rd Edition, Prentice Hall

Schein, E. (2004) *Organisational Change and Leadership,* Pfeiffer Wiley

Senn Delaney Leadership, (2000) *Leadership, Team Building, Culture Change*

Semler, R. (1993) *Maverick!*, Random House

Spector, R. (2000) *Amazon.com, Get Big Fast*, Random House

Tannenbaum, R. and Schmidt, W. (1991), *How to choose a leadership pattern, Business classics; Fifteen Key Concepts for Managerial Success*, Harvard Business Review

Turknett, C. and Hitchcock, S. (1998), *Culture, the Competitive Advantage,* HR Atlanta

Whitmore, Sir J. (1992) *Coaching for performance*, Nicholas Brealey Publishing

Yukl, G. (1998) *Leadership in Organisations* (4th edition), Prentice Hall

Zenger, J., Ulrich, D. and Smallwood, N. (2000) The new leadership development, *Training and development*, March 2000